Anna Anon

@chefannaanon

www.annaanon.com

This ain't your regular cookbook, and I sure as hell ain't your run-of-the-mill cook. You won't find me flashing a goofy grin on your television screen or scribbling my culinary escapades in some trendy blog — and let me assure you, that's no accident. My identity is shrouded in secrecy, and there's even speculation over whether I'm flesh and blood. Ironic questions coming from those dealing in fiat, asking for authenticity while their own lives dance in the realm of make-believe.

But here's the real deal — I'm just like you, a culinary maestro in my own kitchen, an anonymous cook, driven by a passion for exceptional food, and a drive for freedom.

Amidst the overwhelming screech of celebrity chefs and social media sensations, I represent the silent majority, an unknown culinary enthusiast, with a singular desire — to cook up one hell of a revolution.

Introduction

Gazing across my cold, barren apartment, the soft hum from my humble mining rig echoed off the empty walls. The dim glow of the monitor feebly lighting the sparse room, illuminating the stark reality of the life I'd chosen. The bear market has its claws out, and my once lavish existence has dwindled to a mere flicker.

It's 2am, and a persistent hunger has been gnawing at me — subtle, but always there. The fridge emits its usual creak, revealing only remnants of better days. A solitary light spills over wilted vegetables and yesterdays pizza box. But in the world of crypto, where markets dip and soar unpredictably, resilience had become second nature. I refuse to let my taste buds succumb to the bear's gloom.

With determination, I salvage the leftover pizza from the fridge. In this moment, little did I know, my true culinary calling was just beginning.

I grab the pan, turn on the stove, and spark the gas burner to life. I set out, using what knowledge I'd built up over the years. I was no stranger to the culinary landscape, from indulging in Michelin-starred restaurants to savoring street food, attending borrels, and enjoying tapas. I'd not only tasted the lifestyle, but cooked and immersed myself in it...and now it was all flooding back.

In every country I'd lived or visited, food functioned as a salvage, an escape, a refuge — a small piece of freedom in the face of hardship. It was the one constant that couldn't be taken. Food connected the people, the recipes living forever amongst them, passed down through generations. An unbreakable network of people, lives, knowledge and cultures, across time, all united by the universal language of flavor.

Today, amidst the era of 5-minute meals, trendy crash diets, and on-demand delivery, one might assume that real culinary culture is on the decline. However, the underlying passion that unites food and people across generations, is not just surviving, it's thriving.

In the midst of the cold, dark, and uncertain bear market of my own despair, I sought all this, and more. I combined my passions, the unbreakable bond of food that I had witnessed, with my drive for for an unbreakable, truely hard form of money.

Little did I realize how seamlessly they would pair. It was a match made in heaven, not only helping me through the winterish market draw downs, but my cooking took on a whole new meaning.

At this point, there was no turning back. I hung up my fiat-apron and stepped away from my fellow fiat-chefs, becoming the world's first 'Bitcoin Chef.'

The recipes, and my cooking, which was always filledwith heart and soul, were now accompanied by one extra thing: Bitcoin.

It became my secret ingredient! Alone, it can be a difficult pill to swallow... Not just understanding it yourself, but trying to explain it to friends, loved ones and those you don't want left behind as their currency loses its flavor.

But these recipes, wrapped in the freedom loving ideas of Bitcoin, were exactly what I needed to drive adoption and win hearts over. It's what propelled me in my journey, and now it's yours.

This book is your culinary companion, offering recipes to weather the markets, build your resilience and embrace the life-altering spirit of Bitcoin. Each dish, a chapter in the saga of my journey, telling a story of survival, growth, and the intoxicating dance of flavors in a world governed by bits and bytes.

Follow along with me, and embark on your own journey, where flavor drives adoption, and hopefully, adoption fuels the evolution of these very recipes. That's the plan!

Together we will craft each dish, learning yummy facts along the way. From my Bear Market's humble reheatings to the Bull Market's extravagant feasts, every page promises a unique take on Bitcoin and the culinary world.

So get ready for one of the most significant orange pillings the world has ever seen, one tasty bite at a time...

Timeless Cooking...

Tick, tock... the familiar mantra echoes in the Bitcoin community.

As the world crumbles, politicians clamor, and corruption prevails, Bitcoin persists—an unwavering force. Regardless of emotions, thoughts, or actions, new blocks meticulously record transactions onto the blockchain, like clockwork. Always adding, always advancing, akin to the relentless march of time, new blocks are minted approximately every 10 minutes.

This perpetual addition to the blockchain mirrors the evolution of Bitcoin itself. Technologies, layering upon one another, built up over time. Moreover, it resembles the creation of extraordinary dishes. Recipes are refined, perfected, and passed down through the ages, with each generation building upon the culinary foundations laid before. This timeless process has unfolded over millennia, shaping not only our taste buds but also the very culinary creations we continue to enhance and expand upon.

I invite you to share your culinary creations not only with family and friends, but with the world, using the hashtag **#CookingWithBitcoin**

When it comes to crafting these delectable meals, conventional measures of time fades away, for these dishes transcend the notion of minutes. Instead, we turn to the building blocks — the blocks of the Bitcoin blockchain itself.

In assessing the duration of a recipe, from beginning to completion, cast your gaze upon the block time. A block time of 3 equates to 30 minutes, while 7 signifies that your scrumptious meal will be ready within 70 minutes... it's as straightforward as that. We make the dishes, we learn, we improve on them, always moving forward. Tick, tock, another block.

Bulls & Bears

IIn this culinary journey, you won't find a dollar sign gracing the pages. To anchor the cost of crafting these nourishing dishes to an overcooked and crumbling currency would leave a bad taste.

Instead, we delve into the realm of bear and bull terminology—the ebbs and flows that Bitcoin, at least in its infancy, undergoes.

Instead, we delve into the realm of bear and bull terminology — the ebbs and flows that Bitcoin, at least in its infancy, undergoes.

Recipes that proudly wear the bear sign are wallet-friendly, designed for year-round enjoyment, and crafted to be gentle on your budget. Yet, in the face of a weakening dollar and escalating living costs for those in the fiat realm, take this affordability with a grain of salt.

On the other side of the spectrum, our bull-marked recipes embrace opulence. With costly ingredients, they align with prosperous times — akin to the roaring '20s, where fortunes seem to be only up, and indulgence knows no bounds. Unleash the champagne, delicately apply that gold leaf, for this is dining fit for kings.

Of course, some meals fall in between these two extremes and carry a medium rating.

Consider these ratings a rough guide. Access the ingredient costs yourself, and hopefully, no matter what the market is doing or where your life is at, there's good food to be had for all.

With that said, lets get started, the revolution awaits!

What's on the menu...

Bitcoin Bangers 8
Hash Browns 10
Mt. Gox Melts 12
Smashed Savings 14
36-Block Bircher 16
Benedict Standard 18
Bite Sized Bruschetta 20
Ramen Rebellion 22
Satoshi Salad 24
Cryptic Quiche 26
Consensus Curry 28
Budget Burritos 30
Burrata Bounty 32
Aranchini Anonymous 34
Bitties 36
Blockchain Baguette 38
Crostini Chain 40
Digital Dumplings 42
Whale Wallet Wontons 44
God Candle Galette 46
Poor Boy 48
Crypto Pockets 50
Altcoin Almond Energy Bites 52
Running Bitcoin 54
Crypto Ceasar Wrap 56
Sausage Rollups 58
Diamond Hands Skewers 60
Forked Frittata 62
Sovereign Spanakopita 64
Fiat-free Falafel 66
Deciphered Dip 68
LFG Stacked Nachos 70
Quantum Quinoa 72
Crypto Carbonara 74
Private-Key Pesto Pasta 76
Fiatuccine Alfredo 78
Lasagne-256 80
Byzantine Burger 82
Shitcoin Surprise 84
Dough 86
Blockchain BBQ 88
Mining Margherita 90
The Halving 92
Hodlers Reheated 94
Saffron Pilaf à la Silk Road 96
Risotto Reward 98
Segwit Scallops 100
Bullish Beef Pie 102
Token Tandoori 104
Decentralised Duck 106
Proof of Steak 108
Fomo Fondue 110

Drinks & Desserts...

Decentralized Daiquiri	112
Punch Protocol	114
Nakamojito	116
Pina Coinlada	118
Another Fine Mes	120
SATini	122
Trustless Tiki	124
Token Tonic	126
Old Fashioned	128
Dollar Milkshake	130
Hodl Chocolate	132
Lemon Ledger	134
Mining Rig Muffins	136
Cryptic Ice Cream	138
Fat Stacks	140
Bearmarket-Blueberry Cheesecake	142
Peer to Pear Parfait	146
Bitcoin Volcano Cake	148
NFT Nutella Bars	150
Champagne, Truffle & Gold	152
Mooncakes	154
Proof of Work	156

Bitcoin Bangers

Ingredients

- 4 pork or beef sausages
- 2-4 slices of white bread
- 2 cups mashed potatoes
- 4 whole tomatoes on the vine
- Fresh rosemary sprigs
- Olive oil
- Salt and pepper to taste

Cost
Bear Market

Time
2 Blocks

Difficulty
Easy

Introduction

In the world of culinary marvels, simplicity often takes center stage. Nowhere is this philosophy better exemplified than in the backyards of Australia, where a humble sausage finds its perfect companion in a piece of sliced bread.The laid-back Aussies have mastered the art of unpretentious, yet satisfying, meals, with this humble combination pretty much standing as a national dish. Enter Bitcoin Bangers, a nod to the straightforward brilliance of this Aussie classic and a reminder that simplicity is where the value lies. Built on foundations that have held true over thousands of years, Bitcoin's fixed money supply stands as an example of such simplicity. Amid everyone's unique interpretations and spins, simply sticking to the simplicity, in many ways, is all that's needed.

Method

Start by cutting your potatoes into even chunks. Cook in salted water until fork-tender (15-20 mins).

Preheat your grill or grill pan to medium-high heat, and grill the sausages until they are cooked through and have a delicious char on the outside. This usually takes about 10-15 minutes, turning occasionally.

While the sausages are grilling, place the whole tomatoes on the grill. Allow them to char and soften, turning them occasionally. This should take about 5-7 minutes.

Toast the slices of white bread to your liking. You can do this on the grill as well.

While the sausages and tomatoes are grilling, finish your potatoes... drain and mash them using a masher or fork.

Mix in butter and milk to taste. Season with salt and pepper, adjusting to preference. Customize with garlic, chives, sour cream, or cheese.

Assemble:
Put a grilled sausage or two on top of each slice of bread.
Add the charred tomatoes and the mash on the side.
Garnish with fresh rosemary sprigs.
Drizzle with a bit of olive oil and season with salt and pepper.
The combination of savory sausages, creamy mashed potatoes, charred tomatoes, and the aroma of rosemary will make this dish a simple, yet delightful experience.

Hash Browns

Ingredients

For the Hash Browns:

- 4 medium-sized russet potatoes, peeled and grated
- 1 small onion, finely chopped
- 2 tablespoons all-purpose flour
- 1 teaspoon salt
- 1/2 teaspoon black pepper
- 1/4 cup vegetable oil (for frying)

For the Garlic Aioli Sauce:

- 1/2 cup mayonnaise
- 2 cloves garlic, minced
- 1 tablespoon lemon juice
- Salt and pepper to taste

Cost
Medium

Time
4.5 Blocks

Difficulty
Medium

Introduction

Much like the intricate hashes securing transactions on the blockchain, these rustic hash browns promise a symphony of flavors, securely transforming humble ingredients into a culinary masterpiece.

Method

1. Prepare the Hash Browns:
a. Grate the peeled potatoes using a box grater. Place the grated potatoes in a clean kitchen towel and squeeze out as much moisture as possible.
b. In a large bowl, combine the grated potatoes, chopped onion, flour, salt, and pepper. Mix well until the ingredients are evenly distributed.
c. Form the potato mixture into rustic-looking patties, pressing them firmly together.
c. Heat vegetable oil in a large skillet over medium-high heat, until it is hot. To check if the oil is hot enough, you can drop a small piece of potato into the oil. If it sizzles and starts browning, the oil is ready.
d. Carefully place the patties in the hot oil and fry for about 4-5 minutes on each side or until they are golden brown and crispy.
f. Remove the hash browns from the skillet and place them on a paper towel-lined plate to absorb excess oil.

2. Make the Garlic Aioli Sauce:
a. In a small bowl, combine mayonnaise, minced garlic, and lemon juice.
b. Mix well until the garlic is evenly distributed throughout the sauce.
c. Season with salt and pepper to taste. Adjust the lemon juice or garlic according to your preference.

3. Serve:
Plate the rustic hash browns and drizzle the garlic aioli sauce over the top or serve it on the side for dipping.

Mt. Gox Melts

Ingredients

- 4 slices of artisanal bread (sourdough, ciabatta, or your choice)
- 8 slices of high-quality ham
- 1 large ripe tomato, thinly sliced
- 2 cups gourmet shredded cheese (Gruyère, aged cheddar, or a blend)
- Butter, softened
- Dijon mustard or mayonnaise for spreading (optional)

Cost
Bear

Time
1 Blocks

Difficulty
Low

Introduction

Savor the taste of resilience, where each bite is a reminder that in the ever-changing crypto landscape, self-sovereignty is the key to avoiding melt-down. Anything less, and you're running against the very essence of true empowerment.

Method

1. Prepare the Bread:
   - Lay out the slices of artisanal bread on a clean surface. Spread a thin layer of softened butter on one side of each slice.
2. Add Condiments (Optional):
   - Spread a thin layer of Dijon mustard or mayonnaise on the non-buttered side of the bread if desired.
3. Layer the Ingredients:
   - On the buttered side of each bread slice, place 2 slices of high-quality ham.
   - Add a layer of thinly sliced tomatoes on top of the ham.
   - Sprinkle gourmet shredded cheese evenly over the tomatoes.
4. Assemble and Cook:
   - Heat a skillet or griddle over medium heat.
   - Once hot, place the assembled sandwiches (buttered side down) in the skillet.
5. Grill to Perfection:
   - Cook each side for about 3-4 minutes or until the bread is golden brown, and the cheese is melted. You can press down on the sandwich gently with a spatula for a crispier finish.
6. Serve:
   - Remove from the pan, let it cool for a minute, slice if desired, and serve hot.
7. Enjoy:
   - Savor the gourmet flavors of your Ham, Cheese, and Tomato Melt with the perfect blend of textures and tastes.

Smashed Savings

Ingredients

- 1 ripe avocado
- Feta cheese
- 2 eggs
- Rustic-style sourdough bread
- Salt and pepper to taste
- Edible flowers for garnish

Introduction

Embrace the irony; if your pockets echo the depths of the bear market, why not humorously confront the situation with a culinary twist? This dish, laden with creamy smashed avocado, crumbled feta, and a perfectly poached egg, atop rustic sourdough, serves as a delicious paradox to the financial challenges of the crypto winter... or a million times worst, your lost savings through inflation. Dare to indulge in the irony, turning a limited budget into a rich and flavorful experience. Welcome to a breakfast that not only defies financial constraints but also tantalizes your taste buds in the most unexpected ways.

Method

1. Smash the Avocado:
    - Scoop the ripe avocado into a bowl. Use a fork to smash it to your desired consistency. Season with salt and pepper to taste.
2. Prepare the Sourdough:
    - Toast the slices of rustic-style sourdough bread to your liking.
3. Poach the Eggs:
    - In a separate pot, bring water to a simmer. Crack each egg into a small bowl. Create a gentle whirlpool in the simmering water and carefully slide the eggs into the center. Poach for about 3 minutes for a soft, runny yolk.
4. Assemble the Toast:
    - Spread the smashed avocado generously over each slice of toasted sourdough.
5. Add Feta:
    - Sprinkle crumbled feta cheese over the smashed avocado layer.
6. Top with Poached Eggs:
    - Carefully lift the poached eggs from the water using a slotted spoon and place one on each slice of toast.
7. Garnish with Edible Flowers:
    - Sprinkle edible flowers over the top for a visually appealing and flavorful touch.
8. Season and Serve:
    - Add a pinch of salt and pepper over the poached eggs. Serve immediately while the eggs are still warm.
9. Enjoy:
    - Delight in the creamy texture of smashed avocado, the savory notes of feta, the richness of a perfectly poached egg, all atop a rustic slice of sourdough bread. The edible flowers not only add a burst of color but also a subtle hint of freshness.

Cost
Bull Market

Time
2 Blocks

Difficulty
Easy

36-Block Bircher

Ingredients

- 1 cup rolled oats
- 1 cup milk (dairy or plant-based)
- 1/2 cup yogurt (Greek or regular)
- 1 tablespoon chia seeds
- 1-2 tablespoons honey or maple syrup (adjust to taste)
- 1 teaspoon vanilla extract
- 1 large apple, grated (with skin on)
- 1/4 cup nuts (almonds, walnuts, or your choice), chopped
- Fresh berries or sliced fruits for topping
- Additional honey or maple syrup for drizzling (optional)
- Yogurt for serving (optional)

Cost
Low

Time
36 Blocks

Difficulty
Easy

Introduction

Patience is a virtue, especially when it comes to crafting the perfect breakfast. This overnight bircher muesli is a testament to this philosophy, requiring a patient embrace of time — 36 blocks, to be precise, or 6-8 hours. In a world where payments should be as instant as the blink of an eye, this 36-Block Bircher takes its sweet time, and trust me, it's worth every delicious moment of anticipation.

Method

1. Combine Ingredients:
- In a mixing bowl, combine rolled oats, milk, yogurt, chia seeds, honey or maple syrup, and vanilla extract. Stir well to ensure all ingredients are evenly mixed.

2. Add Grated Apple:
- Grate the apple (with the skin on) and add it to the mixture. Mix well to incorporate the grated apple into the oats.

3. Chill Overnight:
- Cover the bowl with plastic wrap or a lid and refrigerate the mixture overnight, allowing the oats and chia seeds to absorb the liquid and soften.

4. Toast Nuts:
- In the morning, toast the chopped nuts in a dry pan over medium heat for a few minutes until they become fragrant. Keep an eye on them to prevent burning.

5. Serve:
- Give the overnight bircher muesli a good stir. If the mixture is too thick, you can add a little more milk to achieve your desired consistency.

6. Add Toppings:
- Spoon the bircher muesli into serving bowls or jars. Top with toasted nuts and fresh berries or sliced fruits.

7. Optional Extras:
- Drizzle a bit of honey or maple syrup over the top for added sweetness, and serve with an extra dollop of yogurt if desired.

8. Enjoy:
- Your delicious and nutritious Overnight Bircher Muesli is ready to be enjoyed! This recipe can be easily customized with your favorite toppings such as seeds, dried fruits, or coconut flakes.

Benedict Standard

Ingredients

For Eggs Benedict:

- 4 large eggs
- 2 English muffins, split and toasted
- 4 slices of Canadian bacon or ham
- Salt and pepper to taste
- Chopped chives for garnish

For Hollandaise Sauce:

- 3 large egg yolks
- 1 tablespoon water
- 1 cup unsalted butter, melted
- 1 tablespoon lemon juice
- Salt and cayenne pepper to taste

Cost
Medium

Time
3 Blocks

Difficulty
Medium

Introduction

The Benedict Standard, transcend mere breakfast — it represents value, like the Gold Standard or Bitcoin Standard, it is backed by something of tangible value. A cafe, who delves into breakfast creation, lives or dies on whether the benedict exists in its offerings. Wether they have adopted the Benedict Standard, as that is the starting point, for which all breakfast value is built. Its absent, can deem it's entire network of offerings invaluable. This is where we end our breakfast recipes... master this, as a home chef, and you've mastered breakfast.

Method

1. Poach the Eggs:

- Fill a large, shallow pan with water and bring it to a simmer. Add a splash of white vinegar.
- Crack each egg into a small bowl. Create a gentle whirlpool in the simmering water and carefully slide the egg into the center. Poach for about 3 minutes for a runny yolk.
- Use a slotted spoon to lift the poached eggs out of the water and place them on a paper towel to absorb excess water. Season with salt and pepper.

2. Prepare the Canadian Bacon:

- In a separate pan, lightly fry the Canadian bacon or ham until it's heated through and slightly crispy around the edges.

3. Toast the English Muffins:

- Toast the split English muffins until golden brown.

4. Make the Hollandaise Sauce:

- In a heatproof bowl, whisk together the egg yolks and water. Place the bowl over a pot of simmering water (double boiler) but ensure the bowl doesn't touch the water.
- Gradually whisk in the melted butter, a little at a time, until the sauce thickens.
- Remove from heat and whisk in the lemon juice, salt, and a pinch of cayenne pepper. Adjust seasoning to taste.

5. Assemble:

- Place a slice of Canadian bacon on each toasted English muffin half.
- Carefully place a poached egg on top of each bacon-covered muffin half.
- Spoon the Hollandaise sauce generously over each poached egg.
- Garnish with chopped chives.

6. Serve:

- Serve immediately while the eggs are still warm. Enjoy your delicious Eggs Benedict with creamy Hollandaise sauce and a hint of fresh chives!

Bite Sized Bruschetta

Ingredients

- Baguette
- Fresh roma tomatoes,
- Fresh basil leaves
- Mozzarella cheese, sliced
- Balsamic glaze (crafted in the language of blockchain)

Cost
Bear Market

Time
1.5 Blocks

Difficulty
Easy

Introduction

Experience the epitome of bite-sized elegance with "Bite-Sized Bruschetta." These miniature marvels are not just appetizers; they're a symphony of flavors, where each bite activates your taste buds like the rhythmic dance of zeros and ones in the digital realm.

Method

Prepare the Mini Baguette Slices:
Start by slicing a mini baguette at a 45-degree angle to maximize surface area. This technique ensures an ideal base for the toppings.

Take a halved clove of garlic and rub it gently over each baguette slice. This step infuses a subtle garlic flavor into the bread, enhancing the overall taste.

Lightly Toast the Baguette Slices:
Place the prepared baguette slices on a grill until they achieve a light toasting. This step adds a delightful crunch to the base, creating a perfect balance of textures.

Assemble
Distribute a generous amount of halved or diced fresh tomatoes evenly over each toasted baguette slice.

Crown with Fresh Basil Leaves:
Top each tomato-covered slice with a fresh basil leafs
The aromatic essence of basil adds a refreshing note to the bruschetta.

Add the Mozzarella:
Place a slice of Mozzarella on top of each piece. This layer adds a creamy texture that complements the other elements.

Finish with a Balsamic Glaze Drizzle:
Complete the masterpiece by delicately drizzling balsamic glaze over the assembled bruschetta.

As you savor each "Bite-Sized Briscotta," let the symphony of flavors activate your culinary circuitry creating a sensation that mirrors the rhythmic pulse of zeros and ones in the vast expanse of the digital world.

Ramen Rebellion

Ingredients

- 1 packet of instant 2-minute noodles
- 1 flavor sauce packet (from the noodle pack)
- Chives
- Carrots (optional)
- Boiling water

Cost
ULTRA Bear

Time
1.5 Blocks

Difficulty
Easy

Introduction

Welcome to full-on crypto-winter, where the depths of the bear market have turned your existence into a real-life meme – captured perfectly in this humble dish. I'd love to say this is make-believe, but heck, even if we can't afford gas to cook, who says we can't relish this tasty delight? Put a smile on, for in this winter, nothing can bring us down. Welcome to Ramen Rebellion!

Method

Open the Noodle Packet:

- Tear open the instant noodle packet, leaving the noodles inside the packaging.

Chop Ingredients:

- Chop the chives into small pieces, and any other ingredients you want, eg. thinly sliced carrot

Add Flavor Sauce:

- Open the flavor sauce packet that came with the noodles and pour it directly into the noodle packet. Squeeze and knead the packet to evenly distribute the sauce.

Add the Ingredients:

- Toss in the chopped chives directly into the noodle packet. Mix them with the noodles and sauce.

Let it Sit:

- Allow the noodles and added ingredients to sit for a minute, letting the sauce infuse and the noodles slightly soften.

Serve and Enjoy:

- Enjoy your Ramen Rebellion straight from the packet. This quick and resourceful recipe captures the rebellious spirit of crypto, and our unwavering belief in freedom.

SOMONCAO

Satoshi Salad

Ingredients

For the Salad:

- 1 head of romaine lettuce, washed and chopped
- Bacon
- Day old bread
- 1 large apple, thinly sliced
- 1 chicken breast (optional)

For the Caesar Dressing:

- 1/2 cup mayonnaise
- 1/4 cup grated Parmesan cheese
- 2 tablespoons freshly squeezed lemon juice
- 1 tablespoon Dijon mustard
- 2 cloves garlic, minced
- 1 teaspoon Worcestershire sauce
- Salt and black pepper

Cost
Bear

Time
1.5 Blocks

Difficulty
Easy

Introduction

Just as Satoshi built upon and combined technologies that already existed, to bring Bitcoin into life, so to have we added to the famous ceasar salad, with apple slices... the Satoshi Salad.

Method

For the Salad:
Cook bacon until crispy. Once slightlycooled, you can crumble it.
Cube day-old bread for croutons.
Thinly slice 1 large apple.
Optionally, grill and slice one chicken breast.

For the Caesar Dressing:
In a bowl, whisk together 1/2 cup mayonnaise, 1/4 cup grated Parmesan cheese, 2 tablespoons freshly squeezed lemon juice, 1 tablespoon Dijon mustard, 2 cloves minced garlic, 1 teaspoon Worcestershire sauce. Season the dressing with salt and black pepper to taste.

Assemble

1. Assemble the salad by combining chopped romaine lettuce, crumbled bacon, croutons, apple slices, and optional chicken in a large bowl.
2. In a separate bowl, whisk together the Caesar dressing ingredients until well combined.
3. Pour the dressing over the salad and toss until all ingredients are evenly coated.
4. Serve immediately, enjoying the delightful combination of crisp lettuce, savory bacon, sweet apples, and the flavorful Caesar dressing.

Cryptic Quiche

Ingredients

- 6 slices of bacon, cooked and crumbled
- 1 cup sharp cheddar cheese, shredded
- 4 large eggs
- 1 cup whole milk
- Salt and black pepper to taste
- A pinch of nutmeg (optional)
- 1 package (2 sheets) store-bought shortcrust pastry sheets

Cost
Bear

Time
1.5 Blocks

Difficulty
Medium

Introduction

Unlock the savory secrets of our Cryptic Quiche, where layers of bacon, cheddar, and a cryptic crust converge waiting to be deciphered.

Method

1. Preheat Oven:
   Preheat your oven to 375°F (190°C).

2. Prepare the Quiche Crust:
   If using store-bought shortcrust sheets, follow the package instructions for pre-baking or use pre-baked sheets.

3. Cook Bacon:
   Cut the bacon and cook until crispy.

4. Prepare Quiche Filling:
   In a bowl, whisk together the eggs and milk.
   Add the bacon, shredded cheddar cheese, salt, black pepper, and nutmeg (if using). Mix well.

5. Assemble and Bake:
   Line a pie dish with the shortcrust sheets.
   Pour the quiche filling into the shortcrust-lined dish.
   Bake in the preheated oven for 35-40 minutes or until the quiche is set and the top is golden brown.

6. Serve:
   Allow the Quiche Lauren to cool for a few minutes before slicing.
   Serve warm and enjoy the delightful combination of bacon and cheddar in each bite.

Consensus Curry

Ingredients

For the Green Curry Paste:

- 2 green Thai chili peppers
- 2 cloves garlic
- 1 shallot, chopped
- 1 lemongrass stalk, sliced
- 1-inch piece of ginger, peeled and chopped
- 1 teaspoon ground coriander
- 1/2 teaspoon cumin
- 1/2 teaspoon turmeric
- 1 cup fresh cilantro leaves
- Zest of 1 lime
- 2 tablespoons soy sauce

For the Curry:

- 1 tablespoon vegetable oil
- 1 block firm tofu, pressed and cubed
- 1 large carrot, thinly sliced
- 2 cups fresh spinach leaves
- 1 can coconut milk
- 1 cup vegetable broth
- 2 tablespoons green curry paste
- 1 tablespoon brown sugar (optional)
- Salt to taste

Introduction

Just as the blockchain seeks consensus to validate transactions, our Consensus Curry harmonizes a symphony of flavors, uniting the vibrant spices of Thai cuisine. Served over a bed of white rice, every spoonful is a nod to the cooperative essence found both in the blockchain and on your plate—a unanimous agreement that great taste knows no bounds.

Method

1. Make the Green Curry Paste:

- In a food processor, combine all the green curry paste ingredients. Blend until a smooth paste forms. Set aside.

2. Prepare the Curry:

- Heat the vegetable oil in a large pan or wok over medium heat.
- Add the cubed tofu and cook until golden brown on all sides. Remove tofu from the pan and set aside.
- In the same pan, add a bit more oil if needed. Sauté the sliced carrots until slightly tender.
- Stir in the green curry paste and cook for 1-2 minutes until fragrant.
- Pour in the coconut milk and vegetable broth, stirring to combine.
- Add the cooked tofu back to the pan. Simmer for 10-15 minutes to allow flavors to meld.
- Taste the curry and add brown sugar and salt if needed.
- Just before serving, add fresh spinach to the pan and cook until wilted.

3. Serve:

- Serve the Thai Green Curry over white rice.
- Garnish with additional cilantro or lime wedges if desired.

Cost
Bear

Time
1.5 Blocks

Difficulty
Medium

Budget Burritos

Ingredients

For the Filling:

- 1 pound (450g) beef sirloin, thinly sliced (or substitute with chicken breast or lamb)
- 1 onion, finely chopped
- 2 bell peppers (any color), sliced
- 2 cloves garlic, minced
- 1 teaspoon ground cumin
- 1 teaspoon ground coriander
- 1 teaspoon smoked paprika
- Salt and black pepper to taste
- 1 tablespoon vegetable oil

For the Burrito Assembly:

- Large flour tortillas
- Cooked rice
- Black beans, drained and rinsed
- Shredded lettuce
- Diced tomatoes
- Grated cheese (cheddar or Mexican blend)
- Sour cream and salsa for serving

Introduction

Just like "bitcoin" teaches us to be smart about money, these Budget Burritos are here to show you that eating on a budget doesn't mean sacrificing taste. We get it – being mindful of spending is crucial. That's why I'm showing you how to cook up these burritos that are not only easy on the wallet but seriously tasty. Perfect for those busy days when you need something quick and delicious. Just wrap 'em up, head outside, and enjoy a flavor-packed meal without breaking the bank.

Method

1. Prepare the Filling:

- In a large skillet, heat vegetable oil over medium-high heat.
- Add chopped onions and garlic, sauté until softened.
- Add thinly sliced beef (or chicken/lamb) to the skillet and cook until browned.
- Stir in sliced bell peppers, ground cumin, ground coriander, smoked paprika, salt, and black pepper. Cook until the peppers are tender and the meat is cooked through.

2. Assemble the Burritos:

- Warm the flour tortillas in a dry skillet or microwave.
- Place a generous spoonful of cooked rice in the center of each tortilla.
- Add a portion of the beef (or chicken/lamb) and bell pepper mixture.
- Layer with black beans, shredded lettuce, diced tomatoes, and grated cheese.
- Optionally, add sour cream and salsa according to your taste.

3. Fold and Serve:

- Fold the sides of the tortilla over the filling, then roll it up tightly to form a burrito.
- If desired, grill the burritos on a hot skillet for a minute on each side to give them a golden color and a bit of crispness.

4. Serve:

- Serve the beef (or chicken/lamb) burritos warm, sliced in half if preferred. Garnish with additional salsa, sour cream, and a sprinkle of cheese.

Cost
Bear

Time
1.5 Blocks

Difficulty
Medium

Burrata Bounty

Ingredients

- 1 large burrata cheese ball
- 1ripe tomatoes, halved
- Fresh basil leaves
- Extra virgin olive oil, for drizzling
- Balsamic glaze, for drizzling
- Sea salt and freshly ground black pepper, to taste

Cost
Bull

Time
3 Blocks

Difficulty
Easy

Introduction

Savor the simplicity of "Burrata Bounty," where the art lies in the elegance of restraint. This dish, designed for the discerning palate, demands a step back—no need to crowd it with excess. The star of the show is the burrata, and the secret lies in mastering the delicate dance of simplicity and timing. As you indulge, envision the reward: a creamy bounty, an indulgent moments, the full block rewards all yours.

Method

1. **Prepare Burrata:**
   - Remove the burrata from the refrigerator and let it sit at room temperature for about 30 minutes to achieve the perfect creamy consistency.
2. **Assemble Tomatoes:**
   - Place the halved tomato on a serving platter. Drizzle them with balsamic glaze and sprinkle with a pinch of sea salt.
3. **Place Burrata:**
   - Gently transfer the room temperature burrata to the center of the platter, allowing it to ooze creaminess.
4. **Garnish with Basil:**
   - Place fresh basil leaves on top of the burrata for a burst of herbal aroma and flavor.
5. **Drizzle Olive Oil:**
   - Generously drizzle extra virgin olive oil over the burrata, tomatoes, and basil.
6. **Season to Taste:**
   - Season the entire platter with freshly ground black pepper and an additional pinch of sea salt if desired.
7. **Serve:**
   - Serve this Burrata Bliss Platter immediately, encouraging guests to dig into the oozing burrata with the juicy tomatoes, aromatic basil, and the delightful balance of olive oil and balsamic glaze.

Aranchini Anonymous

Ingredients

For the Risotto:

- 2 cups Arborio rice
- 1/2 cup dry white wine
- 6 cups chicken or vegetable broth, kept warm
- 1 cup grated Parmesan cheese
- 1 cup finely chopped mushrooms (e.g., cremini or shiitake)
- 1 small onion, finely chopped
- 2 cloves garlic, minced
- 2 tablespoons butter
- Salt and black pepper to tast

For the Arancini:

- 1 cup all-purpose flour
- 3 large eggs, beaten
- 2 cups breadcrumbs
- 1 cup mozzarella cheese, cut into small cubes
- Vegetable oil for frying

Cost
Bear

Time
11-14 Blocks

Difficulty
Medium to High

Introduction

Behold the behemoth arancini, direct from the cobbled streets of Sicily, secret delights are harbored within their golden exteriors. Filled with creamy mushroom risotto and a hidden core of molten mozzarella, it symbolizes our appetite for anonymity in financial dealings. These rebellious collosals transcend the plate, carrying a narrative of culinary rebellion and the quest for a more private and flavorful existence.

Method

1. **Prepare the Risotto:**
    - In a large pan, sauté the chopped onions and garlic in butter until translucent. Add the Arborio rice and cook for 2-3 minutes, stirring frequently.
    - Pour in the white wine and cook until it evaporates. Begin adding the warm broth, one ladle at a time, allowing the liquid to be absorbed before adding more. Continue this process until the rice is creamy and cooked al dente.
    - Stir in the grated Parmesan cheese and chopped mushrooms. Season with salt and black pepper to taste. Let the risotto cool completely.
2. **Shape the Arancini:**
    - Take a portion of the cooled risotto in your hand and flatten it. Place a cube of mozzarella in the center and shape the risotto around it to form a large tear-drop-shaped arancino.
3. **Coat the Arancini:**
    - Roll each arancino in flour, ensuring it's evenly coated. Dip it into the beaten eggs and then roll it in breadcrumbs until fully covered. Place the coated arancini on a tray.
4. **Heat the Oil:**
    - In a large, deep pan, heat vegetable oil to 350°F (180°C). You should have enough oil to submerge the arancini.
5. **Fry the Arancini:**
    - Carefully lower the arancini into the hot oil and fry until golden brown, turning them to ensure even cooking. This usually takes about 5-7 minutes. Remove and place them on a paper towel to drain excess oil.
6. **Serve and Enjoy:**
    - Serve the giant mushroom arancini while they're still warm. Cut one open, and you'll find a gooey, cheesy center within the flavorful mushroom risotto.

Bitties

Ingredients

- 6 slices of bread
- 6 large eggs
- 6 slices of bacon, cooked and crumbled
- 1 cup shredded cheddar cheese
- Salt and pepper to taste
- Butter for greasing muffin tin

Introduction

With a slice of bread cradling a perfectly cooked egg, nestled among savory bacon and melted cheese, each bite is a symphony of textures and flavors. Easy to make and impossible to resist, 'Bitties' are here to elevate your mornings with a burst of deliciousness. Get ready to savor the joy of these miniature delights that pack a punch in every bite!

Method

1. **Preheat Oven:**
    - Preheat your oven to 375°F (190°C).
2. **Prepare Muffin Tin:**
    - Grease the cups of a muffin tin with butter.
3. **Cut Out Bread Holes:**
    - Using a round cookie cutter or a glass, cut a hole in the center of each slice of bread. Reserve the bread circles for later.
4. **Place Bread in Muffin Tin:**
    - Gently press each bread slice into a muffin cup, making sure it forms a cup shape.
5. **Add Bacon and Cheese:**
    - Sprinkle a bit of crumbled bacon into each bread cup, followed by a layer of shredded cheddar cheese.
6. **Crack Eggs:**
    - Crack one egg into each bread cup, ensuring the yolk stays intact.
7. **Season:**
    - Sprinkle salt and pepper over each egg to taste.
8. **Bake:**
    - Place the muffin tin in the preheated oven and bake for approximately 15-20 minutes, or until the egg whites are set, and the yolks are cooked to your liking.
9. **Serve:**
    - Carefully remove the bacon and egg in a hole muffins from the muffin tin and serve them warm. The bread circles can be toasted and served alongside or used for dipping.

Cost
Bear

Time
1.5-2 Blocks

Difficulty
Easy

Blockchain Baguette

Ingredients

- 3 1/4 cups (400g) all-purpose flour
- 1 1/4 cups (300ml) warm water
- 1 teaspoon active dry yeast
- 2 tablespoons olive oil
- 1 teaspoon sugar
- 1 1/2 teaspoons salt
- 1 cup pitted olives (a mix of green and black olives), chopped
- Cornmeal (for dusting)

Cost
Bear

Time
18 Blocks

Difficulty
Medium

Introduction

Blockchain Baguette: A testament to strength and unity, each slice embodies the interconnected richness of olives. Enjoy the resilience of this artisanal creation, a powerful blend of flavors and well-kneaded nodes.

Method

1. Activate the Yeast:
   - In a small bowl, combine warm water and sugar. Sprinkle the yeast over the water, stir gently, and let it sit for about 5-10 minutes until it becomes frothy.
2. Prepare the Dough:
   - In a large mixing bowl, combine the flour and salt. Make a well in the center and pour in the activated yeast mixture and olive oil.
   - Mix the ingredients together until a dough forms.
3. Knead the Dough:
   - Transfer the dough onto a floured surface and knead for about 8-10 minutes or until it becomes smooth and elastic. You can also use a stand mixer with a dough hook for this step.
4. First Rise:
   - Place the kneaded dough in a lightly oiled bowl, cover it with a clean kitchen towel, and let it rise in a warm place for about 1-1.5 hours or until it doubles in size.
5. Add Olives:
   - Once the dough has risen, gently punch it down and flatten it on a floured surface. Sprinkle the chopped olives over the dough and knead it again until the olives are evenly distributed.
6. Shape the Baguette:
   - Divide the dough into two equal portions. Shape each portion into a baguette by rolling it and tapering the ends. Place the shaped baguettes on a parchment-lined baking sheet dusted with cornmeal.
7. Second Rise:
   - Cover the shaped baguettes with a kitchen towel and let them rise for another 30-45 minutes.
8. Preheat the Oven:
   - Preheat your oven to 425°F (220°C).
9. Slash the Dough:
   - Just before baking, use a sharp knife to make diagonal slashes on the top of each baguette. This helps the bread expand while baking.
10. Bake:
    - Bake in the preheated oven for 20-25 minutes or until the baguettes are golden brown and have a hollow sound when tapped on the bottom.
11. Cool and Enjoy:
    - Allow the olive baguettes to cool on a wire rack before slicing. Enjoy the wonderful aroma and flavor of freshly baked bread with olives!

Crostini Chain

Ingredients

- Baguette, sliced into 1/2-inch thick rounds
- 8-10 fresh figs, sliced
- 1 cup crumbled feta cheese
- 1/2 cup walnuts, chopped
- Honey, for drizzling
- Fresh thyme leaves, for garnish
- Olive oil, for brushing the baguette slices
- Salt and black pepper, to taste

Cost
Bear

Time
18 Blocks

Difficulty
Medium

Introduction

Just like transaction are added in blocks to the chain, securing the foundation of Bitcoin, each delectable Crostini you craft becomes a savory link in an unbreakable gastronomic chain. Pile them up, as you forge a repeteur of taste and innovation.

Method

1. Toast the Baguette:
a. Preheat your oven broiler or toaster oven.
b. Brush each baguette slice with olive oil and place them on a baking sheet.
c. Toast the slices under the broiler for 1-2 minutes or until they are golden brown and crisp. Keep an eye on them to prevent burning.

2. Assemble the Crostini:
a. On each toasted baguette slice, spread a generous layer of crumbled feta cheese.
b. Top the feta with slices of fresh figs.
c. Sprinkle chopped walnuts over the figs.

3. Drizzle with Honey:
a. Drizzle honey over each crostini, allowing it to cascade over the figs and walnuts.

4. Season and Garnish:
a. Sprinkle a pinch of salt and black pepper over the assembled crostini.
b. Garnish with fresh thyme leaves for a fragrant touch.

5. Serve:
Arrange the Fig and Feta Crostini on a serving platter and delight your guests with this elegant and flavorful appetizer.

Digital Dumplings

Ingredients

For the Filling:

- 1 pound ground pork
- 2 cups finely chopped Napa cabbage
- 3 green onions, finely chopped
- 2 cloves garlic, minced
- 1 tablespoon fresh ginger, grated
- 2 tablespoons soy sauce
- 1 tablespoon sesame oil
- 1 tablespoon rice vinegar
- 1 teaspoon sugar
- Salt and pepper to taste

For the Dumpling Wrapper:

- 1 package of round dumpling wrappers (about 50 wrappers)
- Water for sealing the wrappers

For Dipping Sauce:

- 1/4 cup soy sauce
- 1 tablespoon rice vinegar
- 1 teaspoon sesame oil
- Optional: chopped green onions and sesame seeds for garnish

Introduction

The bits and bites of this dish transcend the traditional, inviting you to savor the fusion of flavors in our 'Digital Dumplings.' Embrace the intersection of culinary artistry, as your taste buds are switched on and you enjoy this binary treat.

Method

1. Prepare the Filling:
   - In a large mixing bowl, combine ground pork, chopped Napa cabbage, green onions, garlic, ginger, soy sauce, sesame oil, rice vinegar, sugar, salt, and pepper. Mix until thoroughly combined.
2. Assemble the Dumplings:
   - Place a small amount of filling (about 1 tablespoon) in the center of a dumpling wrapper. Moisten the edge of the wrapper with water using your fingertip. Fold the wrapper in half, sealing the edges tightly to form a half-moon shape. Pleat the edges for a decorative touch.
3. Repeat:
   - Repeat the process until all the filling is used. Place the assembled dumplings on a tray or plate, ensuring they are not touching to prevent sticking.
4. Cook the Dumplings:
   - Heat a pan over medium-high heat with a bit of oil. Place dumplings in the pan and cook until the bottoms are beautifully golden brown. Add water to the pan, cover, and steam for an additional 5-7 minutes.
5. Prepare the Dipping Sauce:
   - In a small bowl, mix together soy sauce, rice vinegar, and sesame oil to create the dipping sauce.
6. Serve:
   - Arrange the cooked dumplings on a serving platter, allowing the golden-brown bottoms to showcase their delicious flavor. Garnish with chopped green onions and sesame seeds if desired. Serve hot with the dipping sauce on the side.

Cost
Neutral

Time
6-7 Blocks

Difficulty
Medium

Whale Wallet Wontons

Ingredients

For the Filling:

- 1 pound ground pork
- 2 cups finely chopped Napa cabbage
- 3 green onions, finely chopped
- 2 cloves garlic, minced
- 1 tablespoon fresh ginger, grated
- 2 tablespoons soy sauce
- 1 tablespoon sesame oil
- 1 tablespoon rice vinegar
- 1 teaspoon sugar
- Salt and pepper to taste

For the Dumpling Wrapper:

- 1 package of round dumpling wrappers (about 50 wrappers)
- Water for sealing the wrappers

For Dipping Sauce:

- 1/4 cup soy sauce
- 1 tablespoon rice vinegar
- 1 teaspoon sesame oil
- Optional: chopped green onions and sesame seeds for garnish

Introduction

The bits and bites of this dish transcend the traditional, inviting you to savor the fusion of flavors in our 'Digital Dumplings.' Embrace the intersection of culinary artistry, as your taste buds are switched on and you enjoy this binary treat.

Method

1. Prepare the Filling:
    - In a large mixing bowl, combine ground pork, chopped Napa cabbage, green onions, garlic, ginger, soy sauce, sesame oil, rice vinegar, sugar, salt, and pepper. Mix until thoroughly combined.
2. Assemble the Dumplings:
    - Place a small amount of filling (about 1 tablespoon) in the center of a dumpling wrapper. Moisten the edge of the wrapper with water using your fingertip. Fold the wrapper in half, sealing the edges tightly to form a half-moon shape. Pleat the edges for a decorative touch.
3. Repeat:
    - Repeat the process until all the filling is used. Place the assembled dumplings on a tray or plate, ensuring they are not touching to prevent sticking.
4. Cook the Dumplings:
    - Heat a pan over medium-high heat with a bit of oil. Place dumplings in the pan and cook until the bottoms are beautifully golden brown. Add water to the pan, cover, and steam for an additional 5-7 minutes.
5. Prepare the Dipping Sauce:
    - In a small bowl, mix together soy sauce, rice vinegar, and sesame oil to create the dipping sauce.
6. Serve:
    - Arrange the cooked dumplings on a serving platter, allowing the golden-brown bottoms to showcase their delicious flavor. Garnish with chopped green onions and sesame seeds if desired. Serve hot with the dipping sauce on the side.

Cost
Neutral

Time
6-7 Blocks

Difficulty
Medium

God Candle Galette

Ingredients

For the Potato Galette:

- 4 large potatoes, peeled and thinly sliced
- 1/4 cup melted butter
- Salt and black pepper to taste
- Olive oil for brushing

For the Toppings:

- Smoked salmon slices
- Caviar (your choice of type)
- Crème fraîche or whipped cream
- Fresh dill or chives for garnish

Cost
Bull

Time
6-9 Blocks

Difficulty
Medium

Introduction

Decadence has arrived, the caviar is out, and we're riding with the bulls! Behold the God Candle Galette, a meme-worthy dish crafted to celebrate Bitcoin's triumphant surge in price. It's not just a treat; it's a culinary masterpiece that captures the essence of luxury and celebration. Prepare to indulge in layers of golden lace, smoked salmon, caviar, and creamy accents—a feast fit for crypto enthusiasts and fine dining enthusiasts alike. This is not just a dish; it's a symbol of opulence, a toast to the highs, and a celebration of the God Candle's radiant glow in the crypto world.

Method

1. **Preheat Oven:**
   - Preheat your oven to 375°F (190°C).
2. **Prepare Potato Galette:**
   - In a bowl, toss thinly sliced potatoes with melted butter, salt, and black pepper until well coated.
   - Brush a round baking dish or tart pan with olive oil. Arrange the potato slices in an overlapping circular pattern, creating a golden lace effect. Bake in the preheated oven for 30-35 minutes or until the edges are crispy and golden.
3. **Assemble Toppings:**
   - Allow the potato galette to cool slightly before assembling the toppings.
   - Place smoked salmon slices on top of the galette, creating an even layer.
   - Spoon dollops of crème fraîche or whipped cream over the salmon.
4. **Add Caviar:**
   - Sprinkle caviar generously over the crème fraîche or whipped cream, distributing it evenly for a luxurious touch.
5. **Garnish:**
   - Finish by garnishing with fresh dill or chives for a burst of color and flavor.
6. **Serve:**
   - Carefully slice and serve the Potato Galette with Salmon and Caviar. Each bite should be a delightful combination of textures and flavors.

Poor Boy

Ingredients

- 1 box of store-bought Fish Fingers
- Ciabatta bread, sliced
- Rocket lettuce
- Spinach lettuce
- Tomato, sliced

Homemade Aoili:

- 1/2 cup mayonnaise
- 2 cloves garlic, minced
- 1 tablespoon lemon juice
- Salt and black pepper, to taste
- Chilli (optional)

Cost
Bear

Time
2-3 Blocks

Difficulty
Easy

Introduction

Eating from a box doesn't need to be bad! In times when every penny counts, embrace the simplicity and flavor of the Poor Boy. Crafted from store-bought fish fingers, this budget-friendly Po'boy is a testament to delicious creativity on a shoestring budget. With crispy, golden fish fingers, layers of fresh veggies, and a homemade aioli to tie it all together, the Poor Boy is proof that a simple meal can still be rich in taste. Let's turn a humble box into a feast without breaking the bank!

Method

1. Cook the Fish Fingers:
   - Begin by grabbing the fish finger box, and popping those bad boys in. About 4 per sandwich, just follow the instructions on the box until they are crispy and golden brown. Perfect for air fryer!
2. Homemade Aioli:
   - While the fish fingers are cooking, prepare the aioli. In a bowl, mix mayonnaise, minced garlic, lemon juice, salt, and pepper. Consider adding a touch of chili for extra flavor. Chill the aioli if time allows.
3. Prepare the Ciabatta Bread:
   - Slice the ciabatta bread into the desired sandwich size. Toast the bread lightly if preferred.
4. Assemble the Po'boy:
   - Spread a generous amount of aioli on both sides of the ciabatta bread.
5. Layer the Ingredients:
   - On the bottom half of the ciabatta, arrange a layer of rocket lettuce, followed by spinach lettuce.
6. Add the Tomato Slices:
   - Place tomato slices over the lettuce layers.
7. Top with Fish Fingers:
   - Once the fish fingers are cooked, arrange them on top of the tomatoes.
8. Season:
   - Season with salt and black pepper to taste.
9. Complete the Sandwich:
   - Place the other half of the ciabatta on top to complete the sandwich.
10. Serve:
11. Serve the Fish Finger Po'boy immediately. Optionally, cut it in half for easier handling.

Crypto Pockets

Ingredients

- 4 pita pockets
- 1 cup feta cheese, crumbled
- 1 cup halloumi cheese, grilled and diced
- 1 cup mozzarella cheese, shredded
- 1 Lemon
- 1 cup fresh spinach leaves
- 2 tablespoons olive oil
- 1 teaspoon dried oregano
- Salt and pepper to taste
- Semi-Dried Tomatoes (optional)

Cost
Medium

Time
2-3 Blocks

Difficulty
Low

Introduction

Get ready to stuff your pockets with flavor! Packed with three types of cheese and vibrant spinach, these CryptoPockets are destined to become your new culinary obsession.

Method

1. Grill the Halloumi:

- On a hot grill, cook the halloumi until it's nicely grilled on both sides.
- Squeeze fresh lemon juice over the grilled halloumi for enhanced flavor.
- Once grilled, dice the halloumi and set it aside.

2. Prepare the Filling:

- In a bowl, combine crumbled feta, the grilled and diced halloumi, shredded mozzarella, fresh spinach leaves, olive oil, dried oregano, salt, and pepper.
- Toss the ingredients until well combined.

3. Warm the Pita:

- Gently warm the pita pockets in a grill or oven.

4. Assemble the Pita Pouches:

- Carefully open each pita pocket.
- Fill each pita pocket with the cheese and spinach mixture.

5. Grill the Pouches:

- Place the filled pita pouches on the grill for a few minutes.
- Turn the pouches occasionally until the cheeses melt, and the pouches achieve a golden hue.

6. Serve:

- Serve the Crypto-Pita Pouches hot off the grill, savoring the flavorful fusion of traditional Mediterranean ingredients, and the grilled halloumi with a hint of lemon.

Altcoin Almond Energy Bites

Ingredients

- 1 cup almond flour
- 1 cup rolled oats
- 1/2 cup honey
- 1/2 cup almond butter
- 1/2 cup chopped almonds
- 1/4 cup chia seeds
- 1 teaspoon vanilla extract
- A pinch of salt

Introduction

They may not be your crown jewel, but with each delicious bite, you're energized for whatever comes with these; up or down, you'll have the energy to soldier on.

Method

1. In a large bowl, combine almond flour, rolled oats, chopped almonds, and chia seeds.
2. In a separate, microwave-safe bowl, warm the almond butter and honey together until they can be easily mixed, stirring occasionally.
3. Add the warm almond butter and honey mixture to the dry ingredients.
4. Add vanilla extract and a pinch of salt to the mixture.
5. Mix all ingredients thoroughly until well combined.
6. Place the mixture in the refrigerator for about 30 minutes to allow it to firm up.
7. Once chilled, take small portions and roll them into bite-sized balls.
8. Store the Almond Energy Bites in an airtight container in the refrigerator.

Cost
Medium

Time
5 Blocks

Difficulty
Easy

Running Bitcoin

Ingredients

- 1 cup rolled oats
- 1/2 cup nut butter (almond, peanut, or your choice)
- 1/3 cup honey or maple syrup
- 1 cup nuts and seeds (almonds, walnuts, chia seeds, flaxseeds)
- 1/2 cup dried fruits (cranberries, apricots, raisins)
- Dark chocolate chips (optional)
- 1 teaspoon vanilla extract
- Pinch of salt
- 1/2 cup protein powder (whey, plant-based, or your preferred type)

Cost
Medium

Time
15 Blocks

Difficulty
Medium

Introduction

Just as runners rely on protein for recovery and endurance, these bars embody the sustained energy needed for both physical activities and the dynamic world of Bitcoin.

Named in honor of Hal Finney, you can honor Hal's memory by taking part in the Running Bitcoin Challenge, which helps raise money and treatments for ALS.

Method

1. In a large bowl, combine rolled oats, nut butter, honey (or maple syrup), vanilla extract, and protein powder.
2. Add a mix of nuts, seeds, and dried fruits to the bowl.
3. Stir the ingredients until well combined.
4. Line a baking dish with parchment paper and press the mixture evenly into the dish.
5. Optional: Sprinkle dark chocolate chips on top.
6. Refrigerate for a few hours until firm.
7. Once set, cut into bars or squares.

Crypto Ceasar Wrap

Ingredients

For the Caesar Dressing:

- 1/2 cup mayonnaise
- 2 tablespoons grated Parmesan cheese
- 1 tablespoon Dijon mustard
- 1 clove garlic, minced
- 1 tablespoon lemon juice
- Salt and pepper to taste

For the Wrap:

- 1 large whole wheat or spinach tortilla
- Grilled chicken breast, sliced
- Romaine lettuce, chopped
- Cherry tomatoes, halved
- Shaved Parmesan cheese
- Croutons (optional)

Cost
Medium

Time
3 Blocks

Difficulty
Easy

Introduction

Embark on a culinary journey reminiscent of ancient Rome, where emperors once feasted and legacies were written. Our Crypto Caesar Wrap pays homage to the timeless flavors of a classic Caesar salad, a dish that transcends eras. Enjoy a feast fit for a modern-day emperor as you savor each bite, and ponder what the Roman Empire would look like today, if they had discovered Bitcoin.

Method

1. Prepare the Caesar Dressing:

- In a bowl, whisk together mayonnaise, Parmesan cheese, Dijon mustard, minced garlic, lemon juice, salt, and pepper. Adjust the seasoning to your liking.

2. Assemble the Wrap:

- Lay the tortilla flat on a clean surface.
- Spread a generous amount of Caesar dressing over the entire surface of the tortilla.

3. Layer the Ingredients:

- Place slices of grilled chicken breast down the center of the tortilla.
- Add chopped romaine lettuce, halved cherry tomatoes, shaved Parmesan cheese, and croutons if desired.

4. Roll the Wrap:

- Carefully fold in the sides of the tortilla and then roll it up tightly from the bottom, creating a wrap.

5. Serve:

- Slice the Crypto Caesar Wrap in half at a slight angle for a visually appealing presentation.
- Serve immediately and enjoy your delicious, crypto-inspired Caesar Wrap!

Sausage Rollups

Ingredients

- 1 lb (450g) ground pork or sausage meat
- 1 onion, finely chopped
- 2 cloves garlic, minced
- 1 carrot, grated
- 1 tablespoon tomato paste
- 1 teaspoon dried thyme
- Salt and pepper to taste
- 2 sheets puff pastry, thawed
- 1 egg, beaten (for egg wash)
- Poppy seeds for sprinkling

Cost
Medium

Time
4.5 Blocks

Difficulty
Medium

Introduction

Devour our Sausage Rollups – a side-snack crafted for quick, efficient satisfaction without overshadowing the main meal. Just as these bites don't aim to topple your primary feast but stand ready on the side for a swift and fulfilling answer to your hunger, think of crypto rollups similarly. In the vast landscape of blockchain, they operate on the sidechain, seamlessly processing transactions with speed and efficiency, complementing the main blockchain experience without overshadowing it.

Method

1. Preheat the Oven:
- Preheat your oven to 400°F (200°C).

2. Prepare the Filling:
- In a pan over medium heat, sauté the chopped onion and minced garlic until softened.
- Add the ground pork or sausage meat, grated carrot, tomato paste, dried thyme, salt, and pepper. Cook until the meat is browned and cooked through. Allow the filling to cool.

3. Prepare the Puff Pastry:
- Roll out the puff pastry sheets on a floured surface.
- Using a sharp knife, make 4 or 5 cuts along the sides of each sheet to create a striped effect.

4. Assemble the Sausage Rolls:
- Place a generous amount of the cooled sausage filling along the center of each pastry strip.
- Fold the pastry over the filling, alternating sides to create a woven or striped pattern.

5. Seal and Brush with Egg Wash:
- Press the edges to seal the pastry, and place the rolls seam side down on a baking sheet.
- Brush the tops of the rolls with beaten egg for a golden finish.

6. Add Poppy Seeds:
- Optionally, sprinkle poppy seeds over the top of each roll for added texture.

7. Bake:
- Bake in the preheated oven for 20-25 minutes or until the pastry is golden brown and cooked through.

8. Serve:
- Allow the Sausage Rolls to cool slightly before serving. Enjoy these delightful and visually appealing pastries!

Diamond Hand Skewers

Ingredients

- Halloumi cheese, cut into cubes
- Lemon zest
- Freshly squeezed lemon juice
- Olive oil
- Cherry tomatoes
- Fresh basil leaves
- Wooden skewers

Cost
Medium

Time
6 Blocks

Difficulty
Medium

Introduction

Get ready to elevate your culinary game with these tantalizing Diamond Hand Skewers featuring the one-and-only Halloumi. Just like steadfast investments, these skewers are meant to be held tight and savored. So, don't drop the ball, don't trip on the rugs, and keep the conviction unwavering as you skewer these mouthwatering bites. LFG!!!

Method

1. Crafting Diamond Hands Magic: Skewer your halloumi cubes, cherry tomatoes, and fresh basil leaves with the precision of a seasoned investor. Alternate them gracefully onto wooden skewers, creating a symphony of flavors and textures that rival even the most resilient portfolios.
2. Citrus Marinade Alchemy: Enter the realm of culinary alchemy as you whisk together a captivating concoction in a bowl—olive oil, lemon zest, and freshly squeezed lemon juice. This citrusy marinade isn't just a flavor enhancer; it's the secret sauce that transforms these skewers into Diamond Hands Citrus masterpieces.
3. Brushing Brilliance: Arm yourself with a brush, not to paint on canvas but to coat your skewers with the liquid gold of the citrus marinade. As each drop falls, envision the shimmering potential of your culinary creation, much like the sparkle of a precious gem.
4. Searing Success: Heat up the grill or pan, unleashing the sizzle that echoes the excitement of a thriving investment. Lay your skewers gently on the heat, letting the flames work their magic until the halloumi achieves a glorious golden brown—each skewer a testament to your culinary prowess.
5. Unveiling the Diamond Hands Delight: As the aroma of grilled halloumi and citrus dances in the air, present your Diamond Hands Citrus Skewers to the world. It's not just a dish; it's a proclamation of your unwavering flavor and beliefs.

Forked Frittata

Ingredients

- 8 large eggs
- 1/4 cup whole milk or cream
- Salt and pepper, to taste
- 6 slices of bacon, cooked and crumbled
- 1 cup sliced potatoes (pre-cooked or thinly sliced)
- 1/2 cup shredded cheese (cheddar, Gruyère, or your choice)
- Fresh herbs (chives, parsley) for garnish (optional)

Cost
Low

Time
4 Blocks

Difficulty
Easy

Introduction

Just as a blockchain split diverges into unique paths, our Forked Frittata invites you on a new journey of distinct flavors. Loaded with a variety of ingredients, this egg-based dish is perfect for serving up to guests all year round.

Method

1. **Preheat the Oven:**
   - Preheat your oven broiler.
2. **Prepare Ingredients:**
   - Cook the bacon until crispy, then crumble it. If you haven't pre-cooked the sliced potatoes, you can parboil or sauté them until they are partially cooked.
3. **Whisk Eggs:**
   - In a large bowl, whisk together the eggs, milk or cream, salt, and pepper until well combined.
4. **Combine Ingredients:**
   - Add the crumbled bacon, sliced potatoes, and shredded cheese to the egg mixture. Mix well to distribute the ingredients evenly.
5. **Preheat Skillet:**
   - Heat an oven-safe skillet (preferably non-stick) over medium heat. Add a small amount of oil or butter if needed.
6. **Cook on Stovetop:**
   - Pour the egg mixture into the skillet and cook for 5-7 minutes, or until the edges start to set.
7. **Broil in Oven:**
   - Transfer the skillet to the preheated oven and broil for 3-5 minutes, or until the top is golden brown, and the center is set. Keep a close eye to prevent burning.
8. **Garnish and Serve:**
   - Remove from the oven and let it cool slightly. Garnish with fresh herbs if desired. Slice into wedges and serve directly from the skillet.
9. **Optional: Add Fresh Herbs:**
   - Sprinkle with chopped fresh herbs like chives or parsley for an extra burst of flavor and freshness.
10. **Enjoy!**
    - Serve the frittata warm, and enjoy a delicious and hearty meal.

Sovereign Spanakopita

Ingredients

- 1 package (about 10 oz) frozen chopped spinach, thawed and drained
- 1 cup feta cheese, crumbled
- 1 cup ricotta cheese
- 1/2 cup grated Parmesan cheese
- 1 small onion, finely chopped
- 2 cloves garlic, minced
- 1/4 cup fresh dill, chopped
- 1/4 cup fresh parsley, chopped
- Zest of 1 lemon
- Salt and pepper to taste
- 1/2 cup unsalted butter, melted
- FIlo sheets (about 20 sheets)
- Olive oil for brushing

For Tzatziki:

- 1 cup Greek yogurt
- 1/2 cucumber, finely diced
- 1 clove garlic, minced
- 1 tablespoon fresh dill, chopped
- 1 tablespoon olive oil
- Salt and pepper to taste
- Juice of half a lemon

Introduction

Built with luscious filo, the technology layered upon each other is what got us here, got us from under the thumb of control, and standing on our own, self-sovereign and delish as f*ck. This Greek dish is a must-have in every home chef's repertoire.

Method

1. Preheat your oven to 375°F (190°C).
2. In a large mixing bowl, combine the thawed and drained spinach, feta cheese, ricotta cheese, Parmesan cheese, chopped onion, minced garlic, dill, parsley, lemon zest, salt, and pepper. Mix well until all ingredients are evenly combined.
3. Lay out one sheet of filo dough and brush it lightly with melted butter. Place another sheet on top and repeat the process until you have about 4-5 layers.
4. Cut the layered phyllo into strips or squares, depending on your preference.
5. Spoon a small amount of the spinach and cheese mixture onto one end of each strip or square.
6. Fold the filo over the filling to form a triangle, continuing to fold until you reach the end of the strip or square.
7. Place the assembled triangles on a baking sheet lined with parchment paper.
8. Brush the tops of the triangles with olive oil for a golden finish.
9. Bake in the preheated oven for about 20-25 minutes or until the spanakopita triangles are golden brown and crispy.

For Tzatziki:

1. In a bowl, combine Greek yogurt, diced cucumber, minced garlic, chopped dill, olive oil, lemon juice, salt, and pepper. Mix well.
2. Refrigerate the tzatziki for at least 30 minutes before serving to allow the flavors to meld.

Cost
Medium

Time
5 Blocks

Difficulty
Medium

Fiat-free Falafel

Ingredients

- 1 cup dried chickpeas
- 1/2 large onion, roughly chopped (about 1 cup)
- 2 tablespoons finely chopped fresh parsley
- 2 tablespoons finely chopped fresh cilantro
- 3 cloves garlic
- 1 teaspoon cumin
- 1 teaspoon ground coriander
- 1/4 teaspoon cayenne pepper
- Salt and pepper to taste
- 1 teaspoon baking powder
- 4-6 tablespoons all-purpose flour
- Vegetable oil for frying

For Tahini Sauce:

- 1/4 cup tahini
- 2 tablespoons water
- 2 tablespoons fresh lemon juice
- 1 clove garlic, minced
- Salt to taste

Introduction

Indulge in the guilt-free pleasure of "Fiat-Free Falafel," where each bite is a savory escape from the conventional. As these crispy orbs of delight grace your palate, revel in the freedom from the ordinary. Cooking these is a culinary journey where flavor meets innovation —one that transcends traditional boundaries and embraces a world where taste knows no constraints. Savor the revolution, one falafel at a time.

Method

1. **Prepare Chickpeas:**
   - Place dried chickpeas in a bowl and cover with cold water. Allow to soak overnight. Drain.
2. **Blend Ingredients:**
   - In a food processor, combine soaked chickpeas, onion, parsley, cilantro, garlic, cumin, coriander, cayenne pepper, salt, and pepper. Blend until a coarse meal forms.
3. **Add Baking Powder and Flour:**
   - Sprinkle in baking powder and 4 tablespoons of flour. Pulse to combine. Add more flour as needed until the mixture holds together when pinched.
4. **Chill Mixture:**
   - Transfer the mixture to a bowl, cover, and refrigerate for at least 1 hour.
5. **Shape Falafel:**
   - Form the mixture into golf ball-sized balls using your hands.
6. **Fry Falafel:**
   - In a deep pan, heat vegetable oil to 350°F (180°C).
   - Carefully place falafel balls into the hot oil, frying until deep golden brown. Remove and drain on paper towels.
7. **Prepare Tahini Sauce:**
   - In a small bowl, whisk together tahini, water, lemon juice, minced garlic, and salt. Adjust consistency with more water if needed.
8. **Serve:**
   - Serve falafel balls hot with a side of tahini sauce.

Cost
Bear

Time
2 Blocks

Difficulty
Medium

Deciphered Dip

Ingredients

- 1 can (15 ounces) chickpeas (garbanzo beans), drained and rinsed
- 1/4 cup fresh lemon juice (about 1 large lemon)
- 1/4 cup well-stirred tahini
- 1 small garlic clove, minced
- 2 tablespoons extra-virgin olive oil, plus more for serving
- 1/2 teaspoon ground cumin
- Salt, to taste
- 2 to 3 tablespoons water
- Dash of paprika, for garnish (optional)
- Chopped fresh parsley, for garnish (optional)

Cost
Low

Time
4 Blocks

Difficulty
Easy

Introduction

Unlock the journey into the silky indulgence of homemade hummus, crafted from the humble yet versatile chickpea. This velvety blend of flavors promises a delightful experience, jam packed with protein. Whether paired with crunchy pita chips or fresh veggies, this dip transforms any gathering into a flavorful fiesta, inviting you to 'buy the dip' in the world of flavors. Embrace the simplicity and goodness in every scoop, making each dip an opportunity to sieze upon.

Method

1. **Prepare Chickpeas:**
   - If using canned chickpeas, drain and rinse them under cold water. If you have time, you can also remove the skins for an even smoother hummus.
2. **Combine Ingredients:**
   - In a food processor, combine the chickpeas, lemon juice, tahini, minced garlic, olive oil, ground cumin, and a pinch of salt.
3. **Blend:**
   - Process the mixture until smooth. Scrape down the sides of the bowl as needed.
4. **Adjust Consistency:**
   - If the hummus is too thick, add 2 to 3 tablespoons of water, one tablespoon at a time, and blend until you achieve the desired consistency.
5. **Taste and Adjust Seasoning:**
   - Taste the hummus and adjust the seasoning. Add more salt or lemon juice if needed.
6. **Serve:**
   - Transfer the hummus to a serving bowl. Drizzle with extra olive oil and sprinkle with paprika and chopped fresh parsley for garnish if desired.
7. **Enjoy:**
   - Serve the hummus with pita bread, vegetable sticks, or crackers.

LFG Stacked Nachos

Ingredients

- Tortilla chips
- 1 cup shredded cheddar cheese
- 1 cup shredded Monterey Jack cheese
- Black beans, drained and rinsed
- Sliced jalapeños (fresh or pickled)
- Diced tomatoes
- Sliced black olives
- Sliced green onions
- Sour cream
- Guacamole
- Salsa

Introduction

Imagine a mountain of crunchy tortilla chips, blanketed in a glorious fusion of double cheese—cheddar and Monterey Jack—melted to gooey perfection. But that's just the beginning. Stack on a vibrant array of toppings, from zesty jalapeños to juicy tomatoes, we ain't holding anything back here; LFG!!

Method

1. **Preheat the Oven:** Preheat your oven to 375°F (190°C).
2. **Create a Base:** Arrange a layer of tortilla chips on a large baking sheet or oven-safe dish, ensuring they slightly overlap.
3. **First Cheese Layer:** Sprinkle half of the shredded cheddar and Monterey Jack cheeses evenly over the tortilla chips, creating a cheesy foundation.
4. **Build the Layers:** Add a layer of black beans, sliced jalapeños, diced tomatoes, and sliced black olives. These ingredients add texture, flavor, and a burst of color.
5. **Second Cheese Layer:** Sprinkle the remaining cheddar and Monterey Jack cheeses over the nacho toppings, ensuring each chip gets a generous dose of gooey goodness.
6. **Bake to Perfection:** Place the nachos in the preheated oven and bake for about 10-12 minutes, or until the cheese is fully melted and bubbly.
7. **Toppings Extravaganza:** Once out of the oven, scatter sliced green onions over the hot, melty cheese.
8. **Serve with Dips:** Spoon dollops of sour cream, guacamole, and salsa around the edges or into small bowls for dipping.
9. **Enjoy Immediately:** Dive into the cheesy layers while they're hot and gooey. Each bite should be a delightful combination of crunchy chips, melted cheese, and flavorful toppings.

Cost
Medium

Time
2 Blocks

Difficulty
Easy

Quantum Quinoa

Ingredients

For the Quinoa:

- 1 cup quinoa, rinsed and drained
- 2 cups vegetable broth or water
- Pinch of salt

For the Tofu:

- 1 block (about 14 oz) firm or extra-firm tofu, pressed and sliced into cubes
- 1 tablespoon soy sauce
- 1 tablespoon olive oil
- 1 teaspoon dried oregano
- Salt and pepper, to taste

For the Tahini Drizzle:

- 1/4 cup tahini
- 2 tablespoons water
- 1 tablespoon lemon juice
- 1 clove garlic, minced
- Salt, to taste

For the Bowl:

- 1 cup cherry tomatoes, halved
- 1 cucumber, diced
- 1/2 cup Kalamata olives, pitted and sliced
- 1/2 cup red onion, finely chopped
- 1/2 cup feta cheese, crumbled
- 1/4 cup fresh parsley, chopped
- 1/4 cup extra-virgin olive oil
- 2 tablespoons red wine vinegar
- Salt and pepper, to taste

Optional Protein:

- Grilled chicken, chickpeas, or tofu

Optional Garnish:

- 2 tablespoons sesame seeds

Introduction

Dive into the Quantum Quinoa bowl—a nutritious ensemble symbolizing the quantum-resistant nature of blockchain technology. Brimming with healthy ingredients, this bowl isn't just a feast for your taste buds but a celebration of security and sustenance. Every forkful is a journey into a realm where health meets innovation, making it more than just a meal—it's a quantum experience.

Method

Cook Quinoa:

1. In a medium saucepan, combine the quinoa, vegetable broth (or water), and a pinch of salt.
2. Bring to a boil, then reduce the heat to low, cover, and simmer for 15-20 minutes, or until the quinoa is cooked and the liquid is absorbed.
3. Fluff the quinoa with a fork and let it cool.

Grill Tofu: 4. In a bowl, mix the tofu cubes with soy sauce, olive oil, dried oregano, salt, and pepper.

1. Heat a grill pan or skillet over medium-high heat. Grill the tofu cubes for 2-3 minutes on each side, or until they have a nice golden color. Set aside.

Prepare Tahini Drizzle: 6. In a small bowl, whisk together tahini, water, lemon juice, minced garlic, and salt until smooth. Adjust the consistency by adding more water if needed.

Prepare Vegetables: 7. While the quinoa is cooking, prepare the vegetables.

1. In a large bowl, combine the cherry tomatoes, cucumber, Kalamata olives, red onion, feta cheese, and fresh parsley.

Make the Dressing: 9. In a small bowl, whisk together the extra-virgin olive oil, red wine vinegar, salt, and pepper to create the dressing.

Assemble the Bowl: 10. Once the quinoa has cooled, add it to the bowl with the vegetables.

1. Add the grilled tofu to the bowl.
2. Pour the dressing over the quinoa, vegetables, and tofu. Toss everything together until well combined.

Serve and Enjoy: 13. Divide the Mediterranean Quinoa mixture into bowls.

1. Drizzle each bowl with tahini sauce.
2. Optionally, sprinkle sesame seeds on top for garnish.

Cost
Medium

Time
6 Blocks

Difficulty
Medium

Crypto Carbonara

Ingredients

- 300g pasta (spaghetti, fettuccine, etc.)
- 150g pancetta or bacon, diced
- 3 large eggs
- 1 cup grated Pecorino Romano cheese
- 1 cup grated Parmesan cheese
- 3 cloves garlic, minced
- 1/4 teaspoon freshly ground black pepper
- 2 tablespoons extra virgin olive oil

Cost
Bear Market

Time
3 Blocks

Difficulty
Easy

Introduction

Welcome to the heart of Rome, where tradition meets the decentralized allure of "Crypto Carbonara." Originating from the cobbled streets of Italy, this dish pays homage to the revolutionary spirit of cryptocurrency. This recipe, is one of the first things I mastered cooking, and cooking well. And if I can do it, you sure can!

Method

1. Crafting the Pasta:
• Bring a large pot of salted water to boil using 4 quarts of water. Once boiling, add pasta and cook for 8-10 minutes until al dente. Drain pasta and reserve 1 cup of starchy pasta cooking water.

2. Roman Fusion:
• In a large skillet over medium heat, sauté the pancetta or bacon for 5-7 minutes until crispy and browned. Add the minced garlic and sauté for 1 minute more until aromatic.

3. Culinary Alchemy:
•Transfer the hot drained pasta to the skillet and toss to thoroughly combine with the pancetta and garlic. Embellishing each pasta strand with the Roman essence.

4. Crypto Elegance:
• In a small bowl, whisk together the 3 eggs. Then slowly pour the egg mixture over the pasta as you actively toss the noodles. Allowing the egg to gently cook while coating the pasta, forming a smooth, glistening crypto-blended sauce.

5. Empire's End Touch:
• Remove skillet from heat once pasta is fully coated. Mix in 1 cup pasta water, Pecorino Romano and Parmesan until a glossy sauce forms. Crack fresh black pepper over top and finish with a prime drizzle of olive oil. Savor the fusion of old world savory comfort with new world crypto intrigue.

Savor each byte as if Rome had never fallen, as if they too had discovered Bitcoin, and as if they were on the Bitcoin standard. Every bite is a journey through empires, a testament to the timeless fusion of tradition and technology. Enjoy your time-traveling taste adventure with "Crypto Carbonara"!

Private-Key Pesto Pasta

Ingredients

For the Pesto:

- 2 cups fresh basil leaves, packed
- 1/2 cup grated Parmesan cheese
- 1/2 cup pine nuts or walnuts
- 3 cloves garlic, peeled
- 1/2 cup extra-virgin olive oil
- Salt and black pepper to taste

For the Pasta:

- 1 pound (450g) spaghetti
- Salt for boiling water
- Grated Parmesan cheese
- Fresh basil leaves for garnish
- Cherry tomatoes, halved (optional)

Cost
Bear

Time
1.5 Blocks

Difficulty
Medium

Introduction

Some recipes are shared openly, while others are guarded like precious secrets. When people inquire about my Private-Key Pesto Pasta, I'll often glaze over the details. This dish holds the secret to a flavor combination that will have your taste buds doing a happy dance. Brace yourself for a basil-infused haven so delightful that, when pressed for the recipe by curious relatives, you too, might find yourself saying you lost it in a boating accident.

Method

1. Prepare the Pesto:

- In a food processor, combine basil, Parmesan cheese, pine nuts (or walnuts), and garlic.
- Pulse until ingredients are finely chopped.
- With the processor running, gradually pour in the olive oil until the mixture becomes a smooth paste.
- Season with salt and black pepper to taste. Set aside.

2. Cook the Spaghetti:

- Bring a large pot of salted water to a boil.
- Cook the spaghetti according to package instructions until al dente.
- Reserve a cup of pasta water before draining.

3. Combine Pesto and Pasta:

- In a large mixing bowl, toss the cooked spaghetti with the homemade pesto until well coated.
- If needed, add reserved pasta water a little at a time to achieve your desired sauce consistency.

4. Toppings:

- Garnish with grated Parmesan cheese, fresh basil leaves, and optionally cherry tomatoes

5. Serve:

- Serve the Pesto Spaghetti immediately, offering extra Parmesan at the table for those who want an additional cheesy kick.

Fiatuccine Alfredo

Ingredients

- 1 pound (about 450g) fettuccine pasta
- 1 cup (225g) unsalted butter
- 1 cup (240ml) heavy cream
- 1 cup (100g) freshly grated Parmesan cheese
- Salt and black pepper to taste
- Chopped parsley for garnish
- Basil Lead (optional)

Cost
Bear

Time
2-3 Blocks

Difficulty
Low

Introduction

A Fiat dish, how'd this get in here! Immerse yourself in the luscious allure of 'Fiat-ccine Alfredo,' but be cautious – blink, and it's gone. Al' Fredo will turn on you like Michael Corleone, leaving you heartbroken and your dreams undone. Indulge wisely, for in this culinary world, the taste is fleeting, and every bite could bring you undone.

Method

1. Cook the Fettuccine:
   - Bring a large pot of salted water to a boil. Cook the fettuccine pasta according to the package instructions until al dente. Drain the pasta and set aside.
2. Prepare the Alfredo Sauce:
   - In a large skillet, melt the butter over medium heat. Once melted, add the heavy cream, stirring continuously to combine.
3. Add Parmesan Cheese:
   - Gradually whisk in the freshly grated Parmesan cheese, ensuring it melts into the sauce smoothly. Continue stirring until the sauce thickens to your desired consistency.
4. Season and Toss:
   - Season the Alfredo sauce with salt and black pepper to taste. Add the cooked fettuccine to the skillet and the parsley, tossing the pasta in the creamy sauce until well coated.
5. Serve:
   - Transfer the fettuccine Alfredo to serving plates, garnish with a basil leaf on top.
6. Enjoy:
   - Serve the Fettuccine Alfredo immediately while it's hot. Pair it with additional Parmesan cheese at the table for those who want an extra sprinkle.

Lasagne-256

Ingredients

For the Bolognese Sauce:

- 1 pound (450g) lean ground beef
- 1 onion, finely chopped
- 2 cloves garlic, minced
- 1 carrot, grated
- 1 celery stalk, finely chopped
- 1 can crushed tomatoes
- 1/2 cup tomato paste
- 1/2 cup red wine (optional)
- 1 teaspoon dried oregano
- 1 teaspoon dried basil
- Salt & pepper to taste

For the Bechamel Sauce:

- 4 tablespoons unsalted butter
- 1/4 cup all-purpose flour
- 4 cups whole milk, warmed
- Salt, black pepper & nutmeg

Other Ingredients:

- Lasagna sheets cooked according to package instructions
- 2 cups shredded mozzarella cheese
- 1 cup grated Parmesan
- Fresh watercress

Cost
Bear/Bull

Time
9 Blocks

Difficulty
Medium

Introduction

This masterpiece deserves its own night on the weekly calendar. Each bite is a cryptographic symphony of Bolognese richness and creamy bechamel—an encryption of taste that can elevate Monday nights to a whole new dimension.

Method

1. Prepare the Bolognese Sauce:
a. In a large pot, cook the ground beef over medium heat until browned. Drain excess fat.
b. Add chopped onion, minced garlic, grated carrot, and chopped celery. Cook until the vegetables are softened.
c. Stir in crushed tomatoes, tomato paste, red wine (if using), dried oregano, dried basil, salt, and black pepper.
d. Simmer the sauce for at least 30 minutes, allowing the flavors to meld. Adjust seasoning to taste.
2. Cook the Lasagna Noodles:
a. Cook the lasagna noodles according to the package instructions. Drain and set aside.
3. Prepare the Bechamel Sauce:
a. In a saucepan, melt butter over medium heat.
b. Add flour and whisk continuously to form a roux. Cook for a couple of minutes without letting it brown.
c. Gradually add warm milk, whisking constantly to avoid lumps.
d. Continue to cook until the sauce thickens. Season with salt, black pepper, and a pinch of nutmeg.
4. Assemble the Lasagna:
a. Preheat the oven to 375°F (190°C).
b. In a baking dish, spread a thin layer of Bolognese sauce.
c. Place a layer of cooked lasagna noodles over the sauce.
d. Spread a portion of Bolognese sauce over the noodles, followed by a layer of bechamel sauce and a sprinkle of mozzarella and Parmesan cheese.
e. Repeat the layers until you run out of ingredients, finishing with a layer of bechamel sauce and a generous topping of mozzarella and Parmesan cheese.
5. Bake:
a. Cover the baking dish with aluminum foil and bake for 25-30 minutes.
b. Remove the foil and bake for an additional 10-15 minutes or until the top is golden and bubbly.
6. Garnish and Serve:
a. Let the lasagna rest for a few minutes before cutting into squares.
b. Garnish each serving with fresh watercress.

Byzantine Burger

Ingredients

- 1 lb (450g) Angus mince meat
- 4 large burger buns
- 1 cup Gruyère cheese, shredded
- 1 cup mushrooms, sliced
- 1 large onion, thinly sliced
- 4 large potatoes, for the fat-cut chips
- Salt and pepper to taste
- Olive oil for cooking
- Your favorite burger condiments (lettuce, tomato, mayo, ketchup)

Cost
Medium

Time
4-5 Blocks

Difficulty
Medium

Introduction

Unveiling the "Byzantine Burger," a culinary masterpiece that, like the Byzantine Generals facing the challenge of consensus, brings together an array of robust elements in perfect harmony. In this gastronomic strategy, thick Angus mince, Gruyère cheese, and caramelized mushrooms and onions converge to create a burger that triumphs over flavor dissent. Just as the Byzantine Generals sought consensus, savor a burger that unites layers of taste in a delicious accord, a feast fit for those embracing culinary diplomacy.

Method

1. **Prepare the Fat-Cut Chips:**
   - Wash and peel the potatoes, then cut them into thick, rustic chips.
   - In a large bowl, toss the chips with olive oil, salt, and pepper.
   - Spread the chips on a baking sheet and bake in a preheated oven at 400°F (200°C) for about 30-40 minutes or until golden and crispy.
2. **Shape the Angus Mince Patties:**
   - Divide the Angus mince meat into four equal portions and shape them into thick burger patties.
   - Season each patty with salt and pepper.
3. **Cook the Burgers:**
   - In a pan over medium-high heat, cook the burger patties to your preferred level of doneness, approximately 4-5 minutes per side for medium.
   - In the last minute of cooking, top each patty with a generous amount of Gruyère cheese, allowing it to melt.
4. **Caramelize Mushrooms and Onions:**
   - In the same pan, sauté the sliced mushrooms and onions until caramelized and golden brown.
5. **Assemble the Burgers:**
   - Toast the burger buns lightly.
   - Place a Gruyère-topped patty on the bottom half of each bun.
   - Add a generous portion of caramelized mushrooms and onions on top.
   - Top with the other half of the bun.
6. **Serve with Homemade Fat-Cut Chips:**
   - Arrange the golden fat-cut chips on the side.
   - Serve with your favorite burger condiments.

Shitcoin Surprise

Ingredients

- 1 lb (450g) sausage links, sliced
- 4 cups potatoes, peeled and diced
- 2 cups sweet potatoes, peeled and diced
- 2 cups carrots, sliced
- 1 onion, finely chopped
- 2 cloves garlic, minced
- 1 can (14 oz) diced tomatoes
- 4 cups chicken or vegetable broth
- 1 teaspoon thyme
- 1 teaspoon rosemary
- Salt and pepper to taste
- Olive oil for cooking
- Fresh parsley for garnish (optional)

Introduction

This stew promises a surprising gem – the sausage. As you savor the hearty mix of root vegetables, you'll find that every now and then, amidst the ordinary, there's a delicious surprise waiting to be discovered. This stew is hearty, flavorful, and perfect for a comforting meal.

Method

1. In a large pot or Dutch oven, heat olive oil over medium heat. Add the sliced sausage and cook until browned. Remove the sausage from the pot and set it aside.
2. In the same pot, add a bit more olive oil if needed. Sauté the chopped onion and garlic until softened.
3. Add the diced potatoes, sweet potatoes, and carrots to the pot. Stir to combine with the onions and garlic.
4. Pour in the diced tomatoes, including their juice, and add the browned sausage back to the pot.
5. Pour in the chicken or vegetable broth, and add thyme, rosemary, salt, and pepper. Stir well.
6. Bring the stew to a boil, then reduce the heat to low, cover, and simmer for about 25-30 minutes or until the vegetables are tender.
7. Adjust the seasoning if necessary. Serve hot, garnished with fresh parsley if desired.

Cost
Medium

Time
6 Blocks

Difficulty
Medium

Dough

Ingredients

- 2 1/4 teaspoons (1 packet) active dry yeast
- 1 teaspoon sugar
- 3/4 cup warm water (110°F/43°C)
- 2 cups all-purpose flour
- 1 teaspoon salt
- 1 tablespoon olive oil

Cost
Medium

Time
180 Blocks

Difficulty
Medium

Introduction

Pizza holds a special place in Bitcoin's history, having been the first transaction made — 10,000 Bitcoins in exchange for two pizzas. To honor this milestone, we'll be creating the valuable foundation for our pizza masterpieces, the dough representing what Satoshi made us, not just a better money, but perfect money, the taste of freedom we'd always longed for.

Method

1. In a small bowl, combine the warm water, sugar, and active dry yeast. Let it sit for about 5 minutes until it becomes frothy.
2. In a large mixing bowl, combine the flour and salt.
3. Make a well in the center of the flour mixture and pour in the yeast mixture and olive oil.
4. Gradually incorporate the flour into the wet ingredients until a dough forms.
5. Transfer the dough to a floured surface and knead for about 8-10 minutes until it becomes smooth and elastic.
6. Place the dough in a lightly oiled bowl, cover it with a clean kitchen towel, and let it rise in a warm place for about 1-1.5 hours or until it doubles in size.
7. Once the dough has risen, roll it out on a floured surface to your desired thickness.

Now, you can use this dough for your BBQ Chicken and Bacon Pizza or any other pizza variation you prefer.

Blockchain BBQ

Ingredients

- Pizza dough (homemade as in our Dough recipe or store-bought)
- 1/2 cup BBQ sauce
- 1 1/2 cups shredded mozzarella cheese
- 1 cup cooked chicken, shredded or diced
- 1/2 cup cooked bacon, crumbled
- 1/4 cup sliced chorizo (optional)
- Fresh rocket leaves for topping
- Olive oil for brushing

Cost
Medium

Time
3 Blocks

Difficulty
Medium

Introduction

As the blockchain connects people directly, so to will this pizza. Invite your friends over, and cook up a storm with the Blockchain BBQ

Method

1. Preheat your oven to the highest temperature it can go, typically around 475°F (245°C).
2. Roll out your pizza dough on a floured surface to your desired thickness.
3. If using a pizza stone, transfer the rolled-out dough onto a pizza peel or an inverted baking sheet dusted with cornmeal.
4. Spread an even layer of BBQ sauce over the pizza dough, leaving a small border around the edges for the crust.
5. Sprinkle the shredded mozzarella cheese evenly over the BBQ sauce.
6. Distribute the cooked chicken, crumbled bacon, and sliced chorizo (if using) over the cheese.
7. Carefully transfer the pizza to the preheated pizza stone or a baking sheet.
8. Bake in the preheated oven for about 10-12 minutes or until the crust is golden and the cheese is melted and bubbly.
9. Remove the pizza from the oven and top it with fresh rocket leaves.
10. Drizzle with a bit of olive oil before slicing and serving.

Enjoy your delicious Blockchain BBQ Pizza!

Mining Margherita

Ingredients

- Pizza dough (homemade as in our Dough recipe or store-bought)
- Tomato sauce
- Fresh mozzarella cheese, sliced or torn
- Fresh tomatoes, thinly sliced
- Fresh basil leaves
- Olive oil
- Salt and pepper to taste

Cost
Medium

Time
2-3 Blocks

Difficulty
Medium

Introduction

Embark on a culinary with this home made, with this Italian style pizza. Feel the thrill of creating your own masterpiece, mirroring the dedication and precision that make Bitcoin mining a rewarding adventure.

Method

1. **Preheat the Oven:**
   - Preheat your oven to the highest setting (usually around 475-500°F or 245-260°C).
2. **Prepare the Dough:**
   - Roll out the pizza dough on a floured surface to your desired thickness.
3. **Assemble the Pizza:**
   - Place the rolled-out dough on a pizza stone or baking sheet.
   - Spread a thin layer of tomato sauce over the dough.
   - Arrange the fresh mozzarella slices or torn pieces evenly on the sauce.
   - Add the thinly sliced fresh tomatoes.
   - Sprinkle salt and pepper to taste.
   - Drizzle a bit of olive oil over the pizza.
4. **Bake:**
   - Carefully transfer the pizza to the preheated oven.
   - Bake until the crust is golden and the cheese is bubbly and slightly browned, usually around 10-12 minutes.
5. **Finish with Fresh Basil:**
   - Once out of the oven, scatter fresh basil leaves over the hot pizza.
   - Allow it to cool slightly before slicing.
6. **Serve:**
   - Serve your traditional Margherita pizza slices and enjoy the simplicity of classic Italian flavors.

The Halving

Ingredients

For the Pineapple Jalapeño Half:

- Pizza dough
- Tomato sauce
- Mozzarella cheese
- Fresh pineapple chunks
- Sliced jalapeños
- Red onion, thinly sliced
- Fresh cilantro

For the Fig, Prosciutto, and Double Smoked Ham Half:

- Pizza dough
- Olive oil
- Goat cheese
- Fig jam
- Prosciutto slices
- Double-smoked ham slices (optional)
- Arugula (for topping after baking)

Introduction

'The Halving' — a pizza that challenges the norms, much like the infamous Satoshi post suggesting Pineapple and Jalapeños as a delicious topping. While the authenticity of the post was off, the sentiment is clear: everyone has different tastes, and no one should miss out on the rewards of culinary exploration. Build each side, however you'd like! This unconventional pizza embraces the diversity, inviting you to savor the increasing scarcity of Bitcoin, as the difficulty to come across tasty rewards continually halves along its journey.

Method

1. **Preheat the Oven:**
    1. Preheat your oven to the recommended temperature for your pizza dough.
2. **Prepare the Pizza Dough:**
    1. Roll out the pizza dough into two halves.
3. **Assemble the Fig, Prosciutto, and Double Smoked Ham Half:**
    1. Brush olive oil on one half of the pizza dough.
    2. Spread a layer of goat cheese on the oiled half.
    3. Add dollops of fig jam evenly across the pizza.
    4. Lay prosciutto slices on top, ensuring an even distribution.
    5. If desired, add double-smoked ham slices for an additional layer of smokiness.
4. **Assemble the Pineapple Jalapeño Half:**
    1. Spread tomato sauce on the other half of the pizza dough.
    2. Add mozzarella cheese and distribute fresh pineapple chunks, sliced jalapeños, thinly sliced red onion, and chopped cilantro on the second half.
5. **Bake the Pizza:**
    1. Follow the recommended baking instructions for your pizza dough or until the crust is golden and the cheese is melted.
6. **Top with Fresh Arugula:**
    1. After baking, top the Fig, Prosciutto, and Double Smoked Ham Half with a handful of fresh arugula.
7. **Slice and Serve:**
    1. Slice the pizza into wedges, creating a visually striking and flavorful combination.

Cost
Medium

Time
8 Blocks

Difficulty
Medium

Hodlers Reheated

Ingredients

- Leftover pizza slices from the night before
- Dreams (the wilder, the better)
- A dash of optimism
- Pinch of creativity
- Grains of patience (for that extra crunch)
- Laughter (optional, but highly recommended)

Introduction

Yesterday's investment need not go astray... we're in the bearmarket and reheated pizza has made it's way into our food triangle! Reheat with confidence, knowing that your leftover pizza will retain its savory value...

Method

1. Place a non-stick pan on the stove over medium heat.
2. Once the pan is hot, strategically position the pizza slices, crust-side down.
3. Introduce a few drops of water to the pan, ensuring it's away from the pizza slices to generate steam and keep the pizza moist.
4. Cover the pan with a lid to trap the heat and steam.
5. Allow the pizza to heat for 3-5 minutes, or until the cheese is irresistibly melted, and the crust achieves that perfect reheated crunch.

Enjoy your Hodlers reheated pizza, this is how it's done, this is the way,
for WGMI!

Cost
Ultra Bear

Time
1 Block

Difficulty
Beyond Easy

Saffron Pilaf à la Silk Road

Ingredients

- 1 cup basmati rice, rinsed and soaked for 30 minutes
- 2 tablespoons butter or ghee
- 1 onion, finely chopped
- 2 cloves garlic, minced
- A pinch of saffron strands, soaked in 2 tablespoons warm milk
- 2 cups vegetable or chicken broth
- Salt to taste
- Freshly ground black pepper to taste
- Wildflowers for garnish
- Dried lemon slices for garnish

Cost
Bear

Time
5 Blocks

Difficulty
Medium

Introduction

Embark on a culinary journey with "Saffron Pilaf à la Silk Road," a dish that mirrors the rich history of the ancient trade routes. Just as Bitcoin transcends borders in the digital realm, this pilaf, infused with the golden threads of saffron, pays homage to the interconnectedness of cultures. This savory creation brings flavors from distant lands to your table, reminding us that the essence of exploration and trade endures. Enjoy a taste of history, innovation and even our money's rocky start, in every aromatic bite.

Method

1. **Prepare Saffron:**
   - Soak saffron strands in warm milk and set aside.
2. **Saute Aromatics:**
   - In a large pan, melt butter or ghee over medium heat.
   - Add finely chopped onions and sauté until translucent.
   - Add minced garlic and continue sautéing until fragrant.
3. **Add Rice:**
   - Drain the soaked rice and add it to the pan.
   - Stir the rice to coat it evenly with the onions and garlic.
4. **Infuse Saffron:**
   - Pour the saffron-soaked milk over the rice mixture.
   - Gently stir to distribute the saffron evenly.
5. **Add Broth:**
   - Pour in the vegetable or chicken broth.
   - Season with salt and black pepper to taste.
6. **Simmer:**
   - Bring the mixture to a boil, then reduce the heat to low.
   - Cover the pan with a tight-fitting lid and simmer for 15-18 minutes or until the rice is tender and has absorbed the liquid.
7. **Fluff and Garnish:**
   - Once the rice is cooked, fluff it with a fork.
   - Garnish with wildflowers and arrange dried lemon slices on top for a visually appealing presentation.
8. **Serve:**
   - Spoon the saffron pilaf onto a serving platter and enjoy this aromatic and flavorful dish.

Risotto Reward

Ingredients

- 1 cup Arborio rice
- 1/2 cup dry white wine
- 4 cups chicken or vegetable broth, kept warm
- 1 cup mixed mushrooms, sliced (such as cremini, shiitake, or oyster)
- 1 small onion, finely chopped
- 2 cloves garlic, minced
- 2 tablespoons truffle oil
- 1/2 cup grated Parmesan cheese
- Salt and pepper to taste
- Optional: Chili flakes or dried sun-dried tomato flakes for garnish
- Fresh parsley, chopped, for garnish

Cost
Bear

Time
18 Blocks

Difficulty
Medium

Introduction

If you've got a keen nose, you've already sniffed out your reward. Much like securing a block, the truffle within this Risotto makes your culinary effort worth every flavorful bite. Savor the taste of success with this indulgent Rosotto Reward.

Method

1. In a large pan, heat a tablespoon of olive oil over medium heat. Add the chopped onion and garlic, cooking until softened.
2. Add the Arborio rice to the pan, stirring to coat the rice in the oil. Toast the rice for about 2 minutes until it becomes slightly translucent.
3. Pour in the white wine and stir until it's mostly absorbed by the rice.
4. Begin adding the warm broth one ladle at a time, stirring frequently. Wait until the liquid is mostly absorbed before adding the next ladle. Continue this process until the rice is creamy and cooked to al dente texture.
5. In a separate pan, sauté the mixed mushrooms in truffle oil until they are tender and have a golden color. Season with salt and pepper.
6. Once the risotto is cooked, stir in the sautéed mushrooms and grated Parmesan cheese. Adjust the seasoning with salt and pepper.
7. Optional: Serve the risotto garnished with a sprinkle of chili flakes or dried sun-dried tomato flakes for an extra layer of flavor and a touch of color.
8. Plate the risotto, shaving fresh Parmesan on top and finishing with a sprinkle of fresh chopped parsley.

Segwit Scallops

Ingredients

- Fresh scallops (allow 2-3 per person)
- Salt and black pepper, to taste
- 2 tablespoons olive oil
- 1/2 cup Champagne or sparkling wine
- 1/4 cup heavy cream
- 2 tablespoons unsalted butter
- Fresh chives or parsley, finely chopped (for garnish)
- Lemon wedges (for serving)

- 1 cup fresh basil leaves
- 1/4 cup pine nuts
- 1/4 cup grated Parmesan cheese
- 1 garlic clove, peeled
- 1/2 cup extra-virgin olive oil
- Salt and black pepper, to taste

Cost
Bull

Time
3 Blocks

Difficulty
Medium

Introduction

Just as SegWit separates transaction components, these Seared Scallops stand alone on the plate, distinct and distinguished. Although segregated, each bite comes together as a celebration, where the richness of Champagne Sauce and the crisp watercress enhance the unique elegance of each scallops. Experience fine dining and witness the unparalleled elegance of this dish.

Method

Prepare the Scallops:

1. Pat the scallops dry with paper towels to remove excess moisture. Season both sides with salt and black pepper.

Sear the Scallops:

1. Heat olive oil in a skillet over medium-high heat until hot but not smoking. Add the scallops to the skillet, making sure not to overcrowd them.
2. Sear for 1-2 minutes on each side until golden brown and cooked through. The center should still be slightly translucent.

Make the Champagne Sauce:

1. Remove the scallops from the skillet and set them aside. In the same skillet, pour in the Champagne or sparkling wine. Use a wooden spoon to scrape up any browned bits from the bottom of the pan.

Reduce and Add Cream:

1. Allow the Champagne to reduce by half, then add the heavy cream. Simmer for an additional 2-3 minutes until the sauce thickens slightly.

Finish with Butter:

1. Reduce the heat to low and whisk in the unsalted butter until the sauce is smooth and glossy. Season with salt and black pepper to taste.

Basil Pesto:

1. In a food processor, combine basil leaves, pine nuts, Parmesan cheese, and garlic. Pulse until finely chopped.
2. With the processor running, slowly drizzle in the olive oil until the pesto reaches a smooth consistency. Season with salt and black pepper to taste.

Plate the Scallops:

1. Arrange the seared scallops on serving plates. Spoon the Champagne sauce over the scallops.

Garnish and Serve:

1. Garnish with finely chopped fresh chives or parsley.
2. Add small dollops of basil pesto around the plate for both visual appeal and an extra burst of flavor.
3. Serve immediately with lemon wedges on the side, presenting a culinary masterpiece that balances flavors and aesthetics.

Bullish Beef Pie

Ingredients

- 500g beef mince
- 500g beef chunks or cubes
- 1 onion, finely chopped
- 2 cloves garlic, minced
- 2 carrots, diced
- 2 celery stalks, diced
- 2 tablespoons tomato paste
- 1 cup beef broth
- 1 cup red wine (optional)
- 2 tablespoons all-purpose flour
- 2 tablespoons olive oil
- Fresh thyme and rosemary, chopped
- Salt and pepper to taste
- Pastry sheets for pie crust

Cost
Medium

Time
9-12 Blocks

Difficulty
Medium

Introduction

In the realm of both markets and kitchens, being bullish signifies an unwavering confidence. Embrace the bullish spirit with our hearty and comforting Bullish Beef Pie. This culinary creation boasts a harmonious blend of minced beef and tender chunks, enveloped in a golden crust. Just like a seasoned holder, you'll experience a journey of ups and downs creating this, but you'll remain unwavering, and savor the taste of bullish confidence in every delicious forkful.

Method

1. **Preheat the Oven:** Preheat your oven to 180°C (350°F).
2. **Prepare the Filling:** In a large pan, heat olive oil over medium heat. Add onions and garlic, cook until softened. Add beef mince and beef chunks, cook until browned. Stir in flour to coat the meat.
3. **Add Vegetables and Flavors:** Add carrots and celery to the pan. Pour in the red wine if using, and let it simmer for a couple of minutes. Add tomato paste, beef broth, thyme, rosemary, salt, and pepper. Simmer until the mixture thickens.
4. **Assemble the Pie:** Transfer the beef mixture to a pie dish. Roll out the pastry sheets and place them over the filling, trimming any excess. Create slits on the pastry to allow steam to escape.
5. **Bake:** Bake in the preheated oven for about 25-30 minutes or until the pastry is golden brown.
6. **Serve:** Allow the pie to cool slightly before serving. Slice and enjoy your rustic beef pie.

Token Tandoori

Ingredients

- 1.5 lbs (700g) boneless, skinless chicken breasts, cut into large cubes
- 1 cup plain yogurt
- 3 tablespoons olive oil
- 1 tablespoon minced garlic
- 1 tablespoon minced ginger
- 1 tablespoon ground cumin
- 1 tablespoon ground coriander
- 1 teaspoon turmeric
- 1 teaspoon paprika
- 1 teaspoon garam masala
- 1 teaspoon cayenne pepper (adjust to taste)
- Salt and pepper to taste
- Juice of one lemon

For Mint Yogurt Sauce:

- 1 cup plain yogurt
- 1/4 cup fresh mint leaves, finely chopped
- 1 tablespoon fresh cilantro, finely chopped
- 1 tablespoon honey
- Salt and pepper to taste

Introduction

In "Token Tandoori," each succulent bite of Tandoori Chicken mirrors the rich blend of ideas spices and ideas that bought Bitcoin to be. Embrace the fusion of tradition and innovation as this dish is as diverse and robust as the blockchain technology itself.

Method

1. **Prepare Marinade:**
   - In a large bowl, mix together all the marinade ingredients until well combined.
2. **Marinate Chicken:**
   - Add the chicken cubes to the marinade, ensuring each piece is well coated. Cover and refrigerate for at least 2 hours, or preferably overnight.
3. **Preheat Grill:**
   - Preheat your grill or grill pan over medium-high heat.
4. **Skewer Chicken:**
   - Thread marinated chicken cubes onto skewers.
5. **Grill Chicken:**
   - Grill the skewers for 10-15 minutes, turning occasionally, until the chicken is cooked through and has a nice char.
6. **Prepare Mint Yogurt Sauce:**
   - In a small bowl, mix together yogurt, chopped mint, chopped cilantro, honey, salt, and pepper. Adjust the seasoning to your liking.
7. **Serve:**
   - Serve the Tandoori Chicken Skewers with a side of Mint Yogurt Sauce.

Cost
Medium

Time
15 Blocks

Difficulty
Medium

Decentralised Duck

Ingredients

- 1 Wild Duck Breast
- Salt and Pepper to taste
- 2 tablespoons Olive Oil
- Thinly sliced carrots (for garnish)

Honey Glaze:

- 3 tablespoons Honey
- 1 tablespoon Balsamic Vinegar
- 1 tablespoon Soy Sauce
- 1 teaspoon Dijon Mustard

Cost
Bull

Time
7-8 Blocks

Difficulty
Medium

Introduction

"Behold the meal I've forgone many times through the crypto winters. But when you have it, you'll want to snap some photos and share the proof with your friends. This is not just a meal; it's evidence that you've weathered the storm and made it to the next bull market. It's proof of your hard work, it's what secures the network, and brings freedom to the world... Ladies and gentlemen, this is 'Proof of Steak!

Method

Prepare the Duck Breast:

1. Preheat the grill to medium-high heat.
2. Score the skin of the duck breast in a crisscross pattern, being careful not to cut into the meat.
3. Season both sides of the duck breast with salt and pepper.
4. Drizzle olive oil over the duck breast.

Grill the Duck:

1. Place the duck breast on the preheated grill, skin side down.
2. Grill for about 6-8 minutes or until the skin is crispy and golden brown.
3. Flip the duck breast and grill for an additional 4-6 minutes or until the desired doneness is reached.

Make the Honey Glaze:

1. In a small saucepan, combine honey, balsamic vinegar, soy sauce, and Dijon mustard.
2. Heat over medium heat, stirring continuously until the mixture is well combined and slightly thickened.

Finish the Duck:

1. Preheat the oven to 375°F (190°C).
2. Brush the honey glaze over the grilled duck breast.
3. Transfer the duck breast to a baking dish and finish cooking in the preheated oven for about 5-7 minutes or until the internal temperature reaches your desired level of doneness.

Prepare the Carrots:

1. While the duck is finishing in the oven, heat a small pan over medium heat.
2. Add a bit of olive oil and sauté the thinly sliced carrots until they are tender yet still have a slight crunch.

Drizzle and Serve:

1. Slice the duck breast into thin, elegant slices.
2. Arrange the duck slices on a plate, with the sautéed carrots
3. Drizzle the honey glaze over the duck slices and carrots, allowing it to cascade down the plate.
4. Garnish with a few extra carrot slices for added color and texture.
5. Serve immediately, and enjoy the exquisite flavors and sophisticated presentation of this refined dish.

Proof of Steak

Ingredients

- 2 eye fillet steaks (about 8 oz each)
- Salt and black pepper, to taste
- 2 tablespoons olive oil
- 2 cloves garlic, minced (optional)
- Fresh herbs (rosemary or thyme) for garnish (optional)
- Butter for basting (optional)

Cost
Bull

Time
4 Blocks

Difficulty
Medium

Introduction

"Behold the meal I've forgone many times through the crypto winters. But when you have it, you'll want to snap some photos and share the proof with your friends. This is not just a meal; it's evidence that you've weathered the storm and made it to the next bull market. It's proof of your hard work, it's what secures the network, and brings freedom to the world... Ladies and gentlemen, this is 'Proof of Steak!

Method

1. **Bring the Steak to Room Temperature:**
   - Take the eye fillet steaks out of the refrigerator and let them come to room temperature for about 30 minutes. This ensures even cooking.
2. **Preheat the Pan or Grill:**
   - Preheat a skillet or grill pan over high heat. If you're using an outdoor grill, preheat it to high.
3. **Season the Steaks:**
   - Pat the steaks dry with paper towels. Season both sides generously with salt and black pepper.
4. **Cook the Steaks:**
   - Add olive oil to the preheated pan or grill. Place the steaks on the hot surface and cook for 3-4 minutes on each side for medium-rare, adjusting the time based on your desired doneness.
5. **Baste with Butter (Optional):**
   - In the last minute of cooking, you can add a knob of butter to the pan and baste the steaks. This adds richness and flavor.
6. **Add Garlic (Optional):**
   - If desired, add minced garlic to the pan in the last 30 seconds of cooking. Be careful not to burn the garlic.
7. **Rest the Steaks:**
   - Remove the steaks from the pan or grill and let them rest for 5 minutes. This allows the juices to redistribute, keeping the steak moist.
8. **Garnish and Serve:**
   - Garnish with fresh herbs if desired. Slice the steak against the grain and serve immediately.

Fomo Fondue

Ingredients

- 1 clove garlic, halved
- 1 cup dry white wine
- 1 tablespoon lemon juice
- 1/2 pound Gruyère cheese, shredded
- 1/2 pound Emmental cheese, shredded
- 1/2 pound Fontina cheese, shredded
- 1/4 pound extra sharp cheddar cheese, shredded
- 2 tablespoons cornstarch
- 1 tablespoon kirsch (cherry brandy)
- 1/2 teaspoon dry mustard
- A pinch of nutmeg
- Freshly ground black pepper, to taste
- Assorted dippables: Cubes of crusty bread, blanched broccoli florets, apple slices, cherry tomatoes, and cooked sausage slices

Introduction

You don't want to miss this one! Cook up a feast on the side of the ski slopes with 'Fomo Fondue,' a culinary extravaganza that turns every bite into an alpine adventure. Immerse yourself in the rich blend of Gruyère, Emmental, Fontina, and cheddar cheeses, creating a luxurious dip that elevates the experience, making it as unforgettable as the mountain views. Don't let the fear of missing out on this decadent alpine delight linger—indulge in every dip and savor the slope-side celebration.

Method

1. **Rub Pot with Garlic:**
    - Rub the inside of a fondue pot with the halved garlic.
2. **Prepare Cheese Mixture:**
    - In a bowl, toss the shredded Gruyère, Emmental, Fontina, and cheddar cheeses with cornstarch until evenly coated.
3. **Heat Wine and Lemon Juice:**
    - In the fondue pot, heat the white wine and lemon juice over medium heat until it simmers.
4. **Add Cheese Mixture:**
    - Gradually add the cheese mixture to the pot, stirring continuously in a figure-eight pattern until the cheese is melted and smooth.
5. **Add Kirsch and Seasonings:**
    - Stir in kirsch, dry mustard, nutmeg, and freshly ground black pepper. Continue stirring until the mixture is well combined.
6. **Serve:**
    - Place the fondue pot on the table over a fondue burner. Adjust the heat to maintain a gentle simmer.
    - Serve with assorted dippables.

Cost
Bull

Time
2 Blocks

Difficulty
Medium

Decentralized Daiquiri

Ingredients

- 2 oz white rum
- 1 oz fresh lime juice
- 3/4 oz simple syrup
- Ice cubes
- Lime wedge for garnish
- Zest of 1 lime
- Sugar for rimming the glass

Introduction

Just as a blockchain's consensus is distributed, this classic blend of white rum, fresh lime juice, and simple syrup unites flavor and conversation in a decentralized harmony. The sugar-rimmed glass serves as a nod to the decentralized sweetness that elevates every sip. Embark on a libation journey, toasting not only to a well-crafted cocktail but to the spirit of individual elements merging into a harmonious whole. Cheers to a Daiquiri that embodies the decentralized ethos!

Method

1. **Prepare the Glass:**
   - Run the lime wedge around the rim of a chilled glass to moisten it.
   - Dip the moistened rim into a plate of sugar to coat it for a zesty kick.
2. **Mix the Daiquiri:**
   - In a cocktail shaker, combine the white rum, fresh lime juice, and simple syrup.
   - Add ice cubes to the shaker.
3. **Shake it Up:**
   - Shake the ingredients vigorously for about 10-15 seconds to chill the mixture.
4. **Strain and Serve:**
   - Strain the daiquiri into the prepared sugar-rimmed glass.
5. **Garnish:**
   - Garnish with a lime wedge on the rim for an extra burst of citrus freshness.

Cost
Bear

Time
1 Blocks

Difficulty
Easy

Punch Protocol

Ingredients

- 1 box (3 liters) of red goon (cheap red wine)
- 2 cups orange juice
- 1 cup pineapple juice
- 1/2 cup simple syrup (adjust to taste)
- 1 orange, sliced
- 1 lemon, sliced
- 1 lime, sliced
- Ice cubes
- Fresh mint leaves for garnish (optional)

Introduction

Derived from the word 'goon,' meaning cheap wine, this boxed wine, complete with its silver "goon-bag" bladder, houses the most budget-friendly option. Welcome to the bear market, where you don't need to break the bank for your drink to pack a flavor punch!

Method

1. **Prepare the Fruits:**
   - Wash and slice the orange, lemon, and lime into thin rounds.
2. **Mix the Base:**
   - In a large punch bowl, combine the entire box of red goon with the orange juice and pineapple juice.
3. **Sweeten to Taste:**
   - Gradually add simple syrup to the mix, tasting as you go. Adjust the sweetness according to your preference.
4. **Add Citrus Slices:**
   - Drop the sliced oranges, lemons, and limes into the punch for a burst of citrus flavor.
5. **Chill:**
   - Refrigerate the punch for at least 2 hours, allowing the flavors to meld and the mixture to chill.
6. **Serve:**
   - When ready to serve, add ice cubes to the punch bowl.
7. **Garnish:**
   - Optionally, garnish with fresh mint leaves for a touch of freshness.
8. **Enjoy the Protocol:**
   - Ladle the Punch Protocol into glasses and enjoy the budget-friendly, flavor-packed goodness. Perfect for gatherings, especially when embracing the bear market with a taste that hits all the right notes.

Cost
Ultra Bear

Time
1 Blocks

Difficulty
Easy

Nakamojito

Ingredients

- 2 oz white rum
- 1 oz fresh lime juice
- 2 teaspoons sugar
- 8-10 fresh mint leaves
- Soda water
- Ice cubes
- Lime wedge and mint sprig for garnish

Introduction

In the spirit of Satoshi, this classic Mojito has every sip carefully crafted with liberation. Perfect for the hot weather, enter the world of Nakamojito, where the legacy of Satoshi meets the timeless allure of this classic cocktail.

Method

1. **Muddle the Mint:**
    - In a tall glass, muddle the mint leaves with sugar and fresh lime juice. Muddle gently to release the mint's flavor without tearing the leaves.
2. **Add Ice and Rum:**
    - Fill the glass with ice cubes.
    - Pour the white rum over the ice.
3. **Top with Soda:**
    - Top up the glass with soda water, leaving some space at the top.
4. **Stir Gently:**
    - Stir the ingredients gently to combine the flavors.
5. **Garnish:**
    - Garnish the Mojito with a lime wedge and a sprig of fresh mint.
6. **Enjoy the Refreshment:**
    - Sip and savor the refreshing taste of the Classic Mojito in a tall glass, a perfect drink for warm days and vibrant nights.

Cost
Bear to Medium

Time
1 Blocks

Difficulty
Easy

Pina Coinlada

Ingredients

- 2 oz white rum
- 3 oz pineapple juice
- 1 oz coconut cream
- 1 oz heavy cream
- 1 cup crushed ice
- Pineapple slice and maraschino cherry for garnish

Introduction

Inspired by the tropical allure of Piña Colada, this is not just a drink; it's a celebration. Crafted with the perfect blend of white rum, pineapple juice, and coconut cream, each sip takes you on a journey where the legacy of Piña Colada meets the innovation of crypto. Unwind, relax, and savor the Piña Coinlada, where the sweetness of success and the richness of tropical paradise harmonize in every drop. Cheers to a taste of decentralized delight!

Method

1. **Blend Ingredients:**
   - In a blender, combine white rum, pineapple juice, coconut cream, heavy cream, and crushed ice.
2. **Blend Until Smooth:**
   - Blend the ingredients until the mixture is smooth and creamy.
3. **Pour into a Glass:**
   - Pour the blended Piña Colada into a chilled glass.
4. **Garnish:**
   - Garnish with a pineapple slice and a maraschino cherry on top.
5. **Enjoy the Tropical Bliss:**
   - Sip and enjoy the tropical bliss of the Classic Piña Colada, a delightful escape in a glass.

Cost
Medium

Time
1 Blocks

Difficulty
Easy

Another Fine Mes

Ingredients

- 2 oz rye whiskey
- 1 oz reposado tequila
- 1/2 oz orange liqueur
- 1/2 oz Punt e Mes
- 1/4 tsp maple syrup
- 2 dashes Fee Brothers Old Fashioned bitters
- 2 dashes Regan's orange bitters No. 6
- Garnish: Orange twist

Introduction

Sent to the wrong address, rugged and burnt on a sh*t coin—you've stumbled into another fine mess. This recipe pays homage to the pioneers, the trailblazers who discover Bitcoin, endure the hits, and persist. A toast to those navigating the learning curves of self-sovereignty, this drink is crafted in honor of the fine messes we occasionally find ourselves in. Cheers to resilience and the lessons learned on the journey, for to us, we have no other option.

Method

1. Prepare the Mix:
   - In a mixing glass, combine rye whiskey, reposado tequila, orange liqueur, Punt e Mes, and maple syrup.
2. Add the Bitters:
   - Dash in Fee Brothers Old Fashioned bitters and Regan's orange bitters No. 6.
3. Stir and Chill:
   - Stir the mixture well with ice to chill and properly blend the flavors.
4. Strain into Glass:
   - Strain the concoction into a chilled cocktail glass.
5. Garnish:
   - Express the oils from an orange twist over the drink and drop it in as a garnish.
6. Sip and Savor:
   - Take a moment to appreciate the complex interplay of flavors in this Another Fine Mes Remix.

Cost
Medium

Time
1 Blocks

Difficulty
Easy

SATini

Ingredients

- 2 oz gin
- 1/2 oz dry vermouth
- 1/2 oz olive brine (adjust to taste)
- Ice cubes
- Green olives for garnish

Introduction

Shaken, not stirred, and crafted in the spirit of Satoshi's smallest denomination, welcome to the world of the SATini. With each sip of this dirty martini, immerse yourself in the sophistication, where the tiniest details matter just like the smallest satoshis. As you navigate the depths of flavor, consider it a toast to the intersection of timeless elegance and cutting-edge innovation. Cheers to the SATini, where a classic cocktail meets the future of finance.

Method

1. **Chill the Glass:**
   1. Place your martini glass in the freezer or fill it with ice water to chill while you prepare the cocktail.
2. **Prepare the Cocktail:**
   1. In a mixing glass, combine gin, dry vermouth, and olive brine.
3. **Add Ice and Shake:**
   1. Fill the mixing glass with ice and shake the ingredients vigorously for about 15-20 seconds. Shaking helps to chill the ingredients and incorporate a slight froth into the cocktail.
4. **Strain into the Glass:**
   1. Discard the ice from the chilled martini glass.
   2. Using a strainer, pour the shaken mixture into the chilled glass.
5. **Garnish:**
   1. Drop a few green olives into the SATini as a garnish. You can also skewer them on a cocktail pick for a stylish presentation.
6. **Enjoy the SATini Experience:**
   1. Sip and savor the SATini, appreciating the convergence of classic cocktail elegance with a crypto twist. The dirty martini meets the future of finance in this sophisticated libation.

Cost
Medium

Time
1 Blocks

Difficulty
Medium

Trustless Tiki

Ingredients

- 2 oz light rum
- 3/4 oz dark rum
- 1/2 oz orange liqueur (such as triple sec)
- 1/2 oz almond syrup (orgeat)
- 3/4 oz fresh lime juice
- 1/2 oz simple syrup (adjust to taste)
- Crushed ice
- Mint sprig and lime wheel for garnish

Introduction

Served in a distinctive tiki head, this Mai Tai transcends the boundaries of trust, embracing the carefree spirit of tiki culture. Immerse yourself in the tropical symphony of flavors, where every ingredient harmonizes to create a drink as secure and delightful as the blockchain itself. Raise your glass to the trustless future with each sip of this crypto-inspired concoction.

Method

1. **Prepare the Glass:**
   - Fill a tiki mug or old-fashioned glass with crushed ice.
2. **Mix the Mai Tai:**
   - In a shaker, combine light rum, dark rum, orange liqueur, almond syrup, fresh lime juice, and simple syrup.
3. **Shake and Strain:**
   - Shake the ingredients well with ice to chill the mixture.
   - Strain the mixture into the prepared glass over the crushed ice.
4. **Garnish:**
   - Garnish the Mai Tai with a sprig of mint and a lime wheel.
5. **Enjoy the Tropical Escape:**
   - Sip and enjoy the Classic Mai Tai, a tropical escape in a glass with a perfect balance of citrus, almond, and rum flavors.

Cost
Medium

Time
1 Blocks

Difficulty
Medium

Token Tonic

Ingredients

- 2 oz gin
- Tonic water
- Ice cubes
- Fresh lime wedge for garnish

Introduction

Token Tonic, a sip of timeless value in the classic fizz of a gin and tonic. With each effervescent taste, immerse yourself in the simplicity of a traditional cocktail, reimagined for the modern age. Savor not just a drink, but a fusion that bridges the gap between the age-old and the revolutionary. Cheers to Token Tonic—where tradition meets the tokenized future!

Method

1. **Fill the Glass:**
   - Fill a highball glass with ice cubes.
2. **Pour the Gin:**
   - Pour 2 oz of your preferred gin over the ice.
3. **Top with Tonic Water:**
   - Fill the glass with tonic water, leaving some space at the top.
4. **Stir Gently:**
   - Stir the mixture gently to combine the gin and tonic water.
5. **Garnish:**
   - Garnish with a fresh lime wedge on the rim of the glass.
6. **Enjoy the Classic Refreshment:**
   - Sip and enjoy the crisp and effervescent goodness of the Classic Gin & Tonic—a timeless and refreshing cocktail.

Cost
Bull

Time
1 Blocks

Difficulty
Easy

Old Fashioned

Ingredients

- 2 oz bourbon
- 1 sugar cube
- Angostura bitters
- Orange peel
- Large ice cube (made from scratch)
- Additional ice for stirring and serving

Introduction

Rich in history and timeless appeal, this Old Fashioned doesn't need a cheesy name; it's already perfect and built in the eyes of Bitcoin. Inspired by the Manhattan bar in Singapore, where they carve their own ice before your eyes, this drink predates money itself. It's the ledger, the human connection of interacting—unimputable and solid. The Old Fashioned is etched into out code and changes for no one.

Method

1. **Craft the Ice Cube:**
   - Boil water and let it cool to remove impurities.
   - Pour the boiled and cooled water into a large ice cube mold.
   - Place the mold in the freezer and allow the water to freeze completely. This process of boiling and freezing ensures a crystal-clear and denser ice cube, contributing to a slower melting rate and maintaining the integrity of your Old Fashioned.
2. **Prepare the Sugar Cube:**
   - Place the sugar cube in a glass.
3. **Add Bitters:**
   - Soak the sugar cube with a few dashes of Angostura bitters.
4. **Muddle and Stir:**
   - Muddle the sugar cube with the bitters until it dissolves into a paste.
   - Add a splash of water and stir to further dissolve the sugar.
5. **Add Whiskey:**
   - Pour 2 oz of your preferred bourbon into the glass.
6. **Stir with Crafted Ice:**
   - Stir the mixture gently with the crafted ice cube to chill and dilute the drink.
7. **Cut and Ignite the Orange Peel:**
   - Cut a thin strip of orange peel, making sure to include some of the pith.
   - Hold the peel over the drink and give it a firm twist to release the oils.
   - Ignite a lighter a few inches above the drink and squeeze the peel to create a spark, allowing the flame to kiss the surface of the drink briefly.
8. **Discard the Peel:**
   - Drop the orange peel into the glass for added flavor, then remove it.
9. **Serve:**
   - Strain the Old Fashioned into a rocks glass with additional ice.
10. **Enjoy the Expertly Crafted Elixir:**
    - Sip and relish the complexity of flavors in this expertly crafted Old Fashioned, where the art of mixology meets a touch of pyrotechnics.

Cost
Bull

Time
1 Blocks

Difficulty
Medium

Dollar Milkshake

Ingredients

- 2 cups vanilla ice cream
- 1/2 cup shelled pistachios, unsalted
- 1 cup whole milk
- 1/4 cup pistachio-flavored syrup or 2 tablespoons pistachio paste
- Whipped cream (optional, for garnish)
- Crushed pistachios (optional, for garnish)

Introduction

Introducing the "Dollar Milkshake," a Pistachio & Vanilla Milkshake inspired by the theory that, as fiat falters worldwide, the US dollar sucks the value of all other currencies pegged to it. As fiat spirals down, and your milkshake becomes more expensive, we invite you to sit back, relax, and savor the taste of a truly fiat-free world. For at the end of it all, you drink their milkshake.

YOU DRINK THEIR MILKSHAKE!

Method

1. **Prepare the Pistachios:** If your pistachios are not already shelled, remove the shells to get 1/2 cup of shelled pistachios.
2. **Blend the Base:** In a blender, combine the vanilla ice cream, shelled pistachios, whole milk, and pistachio-flavored syrup or pistachio paste. Blend until smooth and creamy.
3. **Check Consistency:** Adjust the consistency by adding more milk if you prefer a thinner milkshake or more ice cream for a thicker texture.
4. **Serve:** Pour the pistachio and ice cream milkshake into tall glasses.
5. **Garnish:** If desired, top each milkshake with a dollop of whipped cream and a sprinkle of crushed pistachios.
6. **Enjoy:** Insert a straw, give it a good stir, and savor the rich and nutty goodness of your Pistachio and Ice Cream Dollar Milkshake.

Cost
Bear

Time
1 Blocks

Difficulty
Easy

Hodl Chocolate

Ingredients

- 2 cups whole milk
- 2 tablespoons cocoa powder
- 2 tablespoons sugar (adjust to taste)
- 1/4 cup semi-sweet chocolate chips or finely chopped chocolate
- 1/2 teaspoon vanilla extract
- A pinch of salt

Cost
Bear

Time
1 Blocks

Difficulty
Easy

Introduction

Sometimes, you just need to sit back, relax, and find comfort in the simple pleasure of holding a warm cup of cocoa. Whether the markets are up or down, it matters you not, for this delightful hot chocolate is a steadfast companion for hodling through.

Method

1. Heat the Milk:

- In a saucepan, heat the milk over medium heat until it's hot but not boiling. Stir occasionally to prevent a skin from forming.

2. Mix in Cocoa Powder and Sugar:

- In a small bowl, mix the cocoa powder and sugar together. Gradually whisk this mixture into the hot milk until it's fully incorporated.

3. Add Chocolate:

- Stir in the chocolate chips or chopped chocolate. Continue stirring until the chocolate is completely melted and the mixture is smooth.

4. Season with Vanilla and Salt:

- Add the vanilla extract and a pinch of salt. Stir well to combine.

5. Serve:

- Pour the hot chocolate into mugs. Top with whipped cream, marshmallows, or chocolate shavings if desired.

6. Enjoy:

- Sip and savor your homemade hot chocolate!

Lemon Ledger

Ingredients

For the Base:

- 1 cup all-purpose flour
- 1/2 cup unsalted butter, softened
- 1/4 cup icing sugar
- A pinch of salt

For the Lemon Filling:

- 4 large eggs
- 1 1/4 cups granulated sugar
- 1/4 cup all-purpose flour
- 1/2 cup freshly squeezed lemon juice (3-4 lemons)
- Zest of 2 lemons

Cost
Bear

Time
1.5 Blocks

Difficulty
Easy

Introduction

In the ledger of knowledge, whether recorded on the blockchain or passed down through recipes, humanity records its story. Just as we add our experiences to the tapestry of time, cooking these Lemon Ledgers becomes a way to tap into our collective knowledge of taste. Add your own spin to the ledger of life – blend tradition with innovation and savor the timeless flavors that echo through the ages.

Method

1. Preheat the Oven:
   - to 350°F (180°C). Grease a square baking pan and line it with parchment paper, leaving some overhang on the sides for easy removal.
2. Prepare the Base:
   - In a mixing bowl, combine the softened butter, icing sugar, and a pinch of salt. Mix until creamy.
   - Add the flour to the butter mixture and mix until a soft dough forms.
   - Press the dough evenly into the bottom of the prepared baking pan.
   - Bake the base in the preheated oven for about 15-18 minutes or until it turns light golden brown. Remove from the oven and allow it to cool slightly.
3. Make the Lemon Filling:
   - In a separate bowl, whisk together the eggs and granulated sugar until well combined.
   - Sift in the flour and whisk again until smooth.
   - Add the freshly squeezed lemon juice and lemon zest to the egg mixture, stirring until well combined.
   - Pour the lemon filling over the slightly cooled base.
4. Bake Again:
   - Place the pan back in the oven and bake for 20-25 minutes or until the filling is set and the edges are golden brown.
5. Cool and Dust with Icing Sugar:
   - Allow the lemon slice to cool completely in the pan. Once cooled, refrigerate for a few hours to firm up the filling.
   - Once chilled, use the parchment paper overhangs to lift the lemon slice out of the pan. Place it on a cutting board and dust the top with a generous amount of icing sugar.
   - Use a sharp knife to cut the lemon slice into squares.
6. Serve:
   - Serve the lemon slices on a plate and enjoy! These are perfect for a refreshing treat with a lovely balance of sweet and tart flavors.

Mining Rig Muffins

Ingredients

- 2 cups all-purpose flour
- 1 cup granulated sugar
- 1 tablespoon baking powder
- 1/2 teaspoon salt
- 1/2 cup unsalted butter, melted
- 2 large eggs
- 1 cup milk
- 1 teaspoon vanilla extract
- 1 1/2 cups fresh or frozen blueberries (if using frozen, do not thaw)

- 1 cup heavy whipping cream
- 2 tablespoons powdered sugar
- 1 teaspoon vanilla extract

Cost
Low

Time
4 Blocks

Difficulty
Easy

Introduction

Step into the world of Mining Rig Muffins, where you don't need to dig deep to find the rewards. Like stumbling upon treasures, the blueberry within these muffins makes them a perfect weekend treat. Let the rich flavors turn your weekend into a delightful mining adventure, as each bite reveals the sweet rewards waiting to be discovered!

Method

1. Preheat the oven to 375°F (190°C) and line a muffin tin with paper liners.
2. In a large bowl, whisk together the flour, sugar, baking powder, and salt.
3. In a separate bowl, whisk together the melted butter, eggs, milk, and vanilla extract.
4. Pour the wet ingredients into the dry ingredients and stir until just combined.
5. Gently fold in the blueberries, being careful not to overmix.
6. Divide the batter evenly among the muffin cups.
7. Bake for 18-20 minutes or until a toothpick inserted into the center comes out clean.
8. Allow the muffins to cool in the tin for a few minutes before transferring to a wire rack.

Whipped Cream:

1. Place a mixing bowl and beaters (or whisk attachment) in the refrigerator for about 15 minutes to chill.
2. Pour the cold heavy whipping cream into the chilled bowl and beat on medium-high speed until soft peaks form.
3. Add the powdered sugar and vanilla extract and continue to beat until stiff peaks form.
4. Be careful not to overbeat; stop as soon as the whipped cream is smooth and holds its shape.

Serve the blueberry muffins warm with a dollop of freshly whipped cream on the side. You can also garnish the whipped cream with a few extra blueberries for a decorative touch.

Cryptic Ice Cream

Ingredients

- 2 cups heavy cream
- 1 cup whole milk
- 3/4 cup granulated sugar
- 1 tablespoon pure vanilla extract
- 1/2 cup shelled pistachios, lightly toasted and chopped

Cost
Bear

Time
24 Blocks

Difficulty
Low to Medium

Introduction

Delve into the frozen and unlock this enigmatic treat, seamlessly blending the timeless allure of vanilla with the rich crunch of pistachios. No ice-cream maker required!

Method

1. **Prepare the Base:**
   - In a mixing bowl, whisk together the heavy cream, whole milk, and granulated sugar until the sugar is completely dissolved.
2. **Add Vanilla Extract:**
   - Add the pure vanilla extract to the cream mixture and whisk again to combine. Ensure the vanilla is evenly distributed.
3. **Chill the Mixture:**
   - Cover the bowl and refrigerate the mixture for at least 4 hours or overnight.
4. **Toast and Chop Pistachios:**
   - Toast the pistachios in a dry pan over medium heat for a few minutes, stirring frequently. Once lightly toasted, let them cool and then roughly chop.
5. **Prepare Whipped Cream:**
   - In a separate bowl, whip the heavy cream until stiff peaks form.
6. **Combine for No-Churn Ice Cream:**
   - Gently fold the whipped cream into the chilled milk mixture until well combined. Add the chopped pistachios and fold again.
   - (If you have an ice cream maker, transfer the combined mixture and follow the manufacturer's instructions for churning.)
7. **Transfer to a Container:**
   - Pour the mixture into a lidded container, spreading it evenly.
8. **Freeze:**
   - Cover with a piece of parchment paper or plastic wrap directly on the surface of the ice cream to prevent ice crystals. Put the lid on the container and freeze for at least 6 hours or until firm.
9. **Serve and Enjoy:**
   - Once fully frozen, scoop the ice cream into bowls or cones and savor the delightful flavors of your homemade Vanilla Pistachio Ice Cream.

Fat Stacks

Ingredients

- 2 cups all-purpose flour
- 2 tablespoons sugar
- 1 tablespoon baking powder
- 1/2 teaspoon salt
- 1 3/4 cups milk
- 1/3 cup vegetable oil
- 2 large eggs
- 1 teaspoon vanilla extract
- Fresh raspberries for topping
- Maple syrup for drizzling
- Whipped cream (optional)

Cost
Bear

Time
2 Blocks

Difficulty
Easy

Introduction

Indulge in the extravagance of breakfast waffles, where every bite is a delicious stack of valuable goodness. Enjoy making these fat-stacks, a decadent tower of fluffy waffles crowned with plump raspberries. Embrace cooking up a feast for your taste buds, in the abundance of both flavor and crypto-inspired joy they bring to your morning ritual.

Method

1. **Preheat Waffle Iron:**
   - Preheat your waffle iron according to the manufacturer's instructions.
2. **Prepare Dry Ingredients:**
   - In a large bowl, whisk together flour, sugar, baking powder, and salt.
3. **Mix Wet Ingredients:**
   - In another bowl, whisk together milk, vegetable oil, eggs, and vanilla extract.
4. **Combine Mixtures:**
   - Pour the wet ingredients into the dry ingredients and stir until just combined. Do not overmix; lumps are okay.
5. **Cook Waffles:**
   - Ladle the batter onto the preheated waffle iron and cook according to the manufacturer's instructions until golden brown.
6. **Assemble Waffle Stack:**
   - Stack the waffles on a serving plate.
7. **Add Raspberries:**
   - Top the waffle stack with fresh raspberries.
8. **Drizzle and Serve:**
   - Drizzle with maple syrup and, if desired, add a dollop of whipped cream.

Bearmarket-Blueberry Cheesecake

Ingredients

For the Crust:

- 1.5 cups graham cracker crumbs
- 1/4 cup granulated sugar
- 1/2 cup unsalted butter, melted

For the Cheesecake Filling:

- 4 packages (32 ounces) cream cheese, softened
- 1.25 cups granulated sugar
- 4 large eggs
- 1 tsp vanilla extract
- 1/4 cup all-purpose flour
- 1 cup sour cream

For the Blueberry Topping:

- 2 cups fresh or frozen blueberries
- 1/2 cup granulated sugar
- 2 tablespoons cornstarch
- 1/4 cup water
- 1 tablespoon lemon juice
- Blueberries & whipped cream

Cost
Medium

Time
1.5 Blocks

Difficulty
Medium

Introduction

Bury those bearmarket blues in this cheesecake that is to-die-for. Dive into a slice of delight, where the sweetness of blueberries meets the creaminess of a classic cheesecake. It's a market of flavors that'll have you trading your worries for another bite.

Method

1. Preheat the Oven:
   - Preheat your oven to 325°F (163°C).
   - Grease the bottom and sides of a 9-inch (23 cm) springform pan.
2. Prepare the Crust:
   - In a bowl, combine cracker crumbs, sugar, and melted butter.
   - Press the mixture firmly into the bottom of the prepared springform pan to form an even crust.
   - Bake the crust in the preheated oven for 10 minutes. Remove and allow it to cool.
3. Make the Cheesecake Filling:
   - In a large mixing bowl, beat the cream cheese until smooth and creamy.
   - Add sugar and continue beating until well combined.
   - Add eggs one at a time, beating well after each addition.
   - Mix in the vanilla extract and flour until just combined.
   - Finally, fold in the sour cream until the batter is smooth.
4. Assemble and Bake:
   - Pour the cream cheese filling over the cooled crust in the springform pan.
   - Smooth the top with a spatula to create an even surface.
   - Bake in the preheated oven for about 50-60 minutes or until the center is set and the top is lightly golden.
5. Cool the Cheesecake:
   - Allow the cheesecake to cool in the oven with the door ajar for about an hour.
   - Refrigerate for at least 4 hours or preferably overnight to set.
6. Make the Blueberry Topping:
   - In a saucepan, combine blueberries, sugar, cornstarch, water, and lemon juice.
   - Cook over medium heat, stirring constantly until the mixture thickens and the blueberries burst, creating a vibrant sauce.
   - Allow the blueberry topping to cool before spreading it over the chilled cheesecake.
7. Serve:
   - Carefully remove the cheesecake from the pan.
   - Top with additional fresh blueberries and a dollop of whipped cream if desired.
   - Slice and serve your delicious Blueberry Cheesecake. Store any leftovers in the refrigerator.

Tokenized Tiramisu

Ingredients

- Ladyfinger cookies (enough to create layers in your serving glasses)
- Cocoa powder, for dusting
- Dark chocolate shavings

For the Coffee Soaking :

- 1 cup strong brewed coffee, cooled to room temperature
- 2 tablespoons coffee liqueur (e.g., Kahlúa), optional
- 2 tablespoons sugar

For the Mascarpone Filling:

- 8 ounces (about 1 cup) mascarpone cheese, softened
- 1 cup heavy whipping cream
- 1/2 cup powdered sugar
- 1 teaspoon vanilla extract

Cost
Low

Time
4 Blocks

Difficulty
Easy

Introduction

This Tiramisu recipe, served in individual portions, becomes the perfect token of taste and indulgence. Elevate your entertaining without the fuss—each serving is elegantly presented in its own glass, eliminating the need for slicing. Delight your guests with the charm of effortless indulgence, where every portion embodies the rich flavors of Tiramisu.

Method

1. **Prepare the Coffee Soaking Mixture:**
   - In a shallow dish, combine the brewed coffee, coffee liqueur (if using), and sugar. Stir until the sugar dissolves. Set aside.
2. **Make the Mascarpone Filling:**
   - In a large mixing bowl, beat the mascarpone cheese until smooth.
   - In a separate bowl, whip the heavy whipping cream, powdered sugar, and vanilla extract until stiff peaks form.
   - Gently fold the whipped cream into the mascarpone until well combined. Be careful not to deflate the whipped cream.
3. **Assemble the Tiramisu Cups:**
   - Dip each ladyfinger into the coffee mixture, ensuring they are soaked but not overly soggy.
   - Place a layer of soaked ladyfingers at the bottom of each serving glass.
   - Spoon a layer of the mascarpone filling over the ladyfingers.
   - Repeat the layers until you reach the top of the glass, finishing with a layer of the mascarpone filling.
4. **Chill:**
   - Cover the glasses with plastic wrap and refrigerate for at least 4 hours or overnight to allow the flavors to meld.
5. **Dust with Cocoa Powder and Garnish:**
   - Before serving, dust the tops with cocoa powder.
   - Optionally, garnish with dark chocolate shavings for an extra touch of decadence.
6. **Serve:**
   - Serve chilled and enjoy your delightful Individual Tiramisu Cups!

Peer to Pear Parfait

Ingredients

- 2 ripe pears, peeled, cored, and diced
- 2 tablespoons unsalted butter
- 2 tablespoons brown sugar
- 1 cup granola
- 1 cup Greek yogurt
- 2 tablespoons honey

Introduction

Introducing the 'Peer to Pear Parfait'—a delightful convergence of caramelized pears, crunchy granola, velvety honey, and luscious Greek yogurt. This parfait isn't just a treat for the taste buds; it's a celebration to be shared, with no intermediaries, enjoyed together, bite by bite.

Method

1. **Caramelize the Pears:**
   - In a skillet over medium heat, melt the butter. Add the diced pears and brown sugar. Cook, stirring occasionally, until the pears are tender and caramelized, approximately 8-10 minutes. Remove from heat and let it cool.
2. **Prepare the Layers:**
   - In each serving glass, create layers using the following sequence:
     - Start with a spoonful of caramelized pears.
     - Add a layer of granola on top of the pears.
     - Spoon in a layer of Greek yogurt over the granola.
     - Drizzle honey over the yogurt.
3. **Repeat Layers:**
   - Repeat the layering process until you reach the top of the glass, finishing with a final drizzle of honey.
4. **Serve:**
   - Serve the pear parfait immediately or refrigerate until ready to serve. The layers will meld together, creating a delightful combination of textures and flavors.

Cost
Bear

Time
2 Blocks

Difficulty
Low

Bitcoin Volcano Cake

Ingredients

For the Chocolate Lava Cake:

- 1/2 cup (1 stick) unsalted butter
- 4 ounces (about 120g) high-quality dark chocolate, coarsely chopped
- 2 large eggs
- 2 large egg yolks
- 1/4 cup granulated sugar
- 1 teaspoon vanilla extract
- 1/4 cup all-purpose flour
- Pinch of salt

For Greasing the Ramekins:

- Butter or cooking spray
- Cocoa powder for dusting

Optional Garnishes:

- Powdered sugar for dusting
- Fresh berries
- Vanilla ice cream

Cost
Medium

Time
3.5 Blocks

Difficulty
Low

Introduction

As Bitcoin paves the way for renewable energies and El Salvador harnesses the power of volcanoes to mine Bitcoin, this dessert pays homage to the sweet advancements towards a greener world. Individual Bitcoin Volcano Cakes, where molten chocolate flows towards a more environmentally conscious future.

Method

1. Preheat the Oven:
   - Preheat your oven to 425°F (220°C).
   - Grease individual ramekins with butter or cooking spray and dust with cocoa powder.
2. Melt the Chocolate and Butter:
   - In a heatproof bowl, melt the butter and chopped dark chocolate together. You can use a double boiler or microwave in 20-second intervals, stirring until smooth. Allow the mixture to cool slightly.
3. Prepare the Batter:
   - In a separate bowl, whisk together eggs, egg yolks, and granulated sugar until well combined.
   - Stir in the vanilla extract.
   - Gradually add the melted chocolate and butter mixture, stirring continuously.
   - Gently fold in the all-purpose flour and a pinch of salt until just combined. Be careful not to overmix.
4. Fill the Ramekins:
   - Divide the batter evenly among the prepared ramekins.
5. Bake:
   - Place the ramekins on a baking sheet and bake in the preheated oven for about 12-14 minutes. The edges should be set, but the center should still be soft.
6. Serve:
   - Carefully remove the ramekins from the oven.
   - Run a knife around the edges of the cakes to loosen them.
   - Invert each lava cake onto a serving plate.
7. Garnish:
   - Dust with powdered sugar, add a scoop of vanilla ice cream, or garnish with fresh berries if desired.
8. Enjoy:
   - Serve immediately and savor the moment as you cut into the warm lava cake, revealing the gooey, molten chocolate center.

These Warm Chocolate Melting Lava Cakes are best enjoyed straight from the oven. Indulge and relish the luscious, molten chocolate goodness!

NFT Nutella Bars

Ingredients

For the Nutella Bars:

- 1 cup (2 sticks) unsalted butter, softened
- 1 cup granulated sugar
- 2 large eggs
- 1 teaspoon vanilla extract
- 2 cups all-purpose flour
- 1/2 cup unsweetened cocoa powder
- 1/2 teaspoon baking powder
- 1/4 teaspoon salt
- 1 cup Nutella (or hazelnut chocolate spread)

For the Chocolate Ganache:

- 1 cup semisweet chocolate chips
- 1/2 cup heavy cream
- Chopped hazelnuts or sprinkles for topping (optional)

Cost
Medium

Time
9-12 Blocks

Difficulty
Low/Medium

Introduction

These indulgent bars, much like the rarest NFTs, bring an exclusive richness to your palate, layering Nutella-infused joy with a chocolatey canvas. Savor the digital delight of these sweet treasures.

Method

1. Preheat the Oven:

- Preheat your oven to 350°F (175°C). Grease and line a baking pan with parchment paper, leaving an overhang for easy removal.

2. Prepare the Nutella Bars Batter: a. In a large bowl, cream together softened butter and granulated sugar until light and fluffy. b. Add eggs one at a time, beating well after each addition. Stir in the vanilla extract. c. In a separate bowl, whisk together flour, cocoa powder, baking powder, and salt. d. Gradually add the dry ingredients to the wet ingredients, mixing until just combined. e. Press about two-thirds of the batter into the prepared baking pan, creating an even layer.

3. Spread Nutella Layer:

- Warm the Nutella slightly to make it easier to spread. Evenly spread the Nutella over the layer of batter in the pan.

4. Add Remaining Batter:

- Drop spoonfuls of the remaining batter over the Nutella layer. Gently spread it as much as possible; it's okay if some Nutella peeks through.

5. Bake:

- Bake in the preheated oven for 25-30 minutes or until a toothpick inserted into the center comes out with moist crumbs, but not wet batter.

6. Prepare Chocolate Ganache: a. In a small saucepan, heat the heavy cream until it begins to simmer. b. Pour the hot cream over the chocolate chips in a heatproof bowl. Let it sit for a minute, then stir until smooth.

7. Pour Ganache Over Bars:

- Once the Nutella bars have cooled slightly, pour the chocolate ganache over the top, spreading it evenly.

8. Optional Toppings:

- Sprinkle chopped hazelnuts or your favorite sprinkles over the chocolate ganache for added texture and decoration.

9. Chill and Cut:

- Allow the bars to cool completely and then refrigerate for at least 2 hours or until the ganache is set. Once chilled, use the parchment paper overhang to lift the bars out of the pan and onto a cutting board.
- Cut into squares or bars.

Champagne, Truffle & Gold

Ingredients

- 200g dark chocolate, finely chopped
- 1/2 cup sweetened condensed milk
- 1 cup champagne or other sparkling wine
- Edible gold leaf for decoration
- Cocoa powder for dusting

Cost
You are the BULL

Time
18 Blocks

Difficulty
Medium

Introduction

Just as Bitcoin was built on the foundations of scarcity, akin to the preciousness of gold, these indulgent orbs are a testament to opulence. Rare and exquisite, I cook them up at the peak of every bull market, and I invite you to indulgein the over the top opulence with each delightful bite.

Method

1. **Prepare the Chocolate Mixture:**
2. Place the finely chopped dark chocolate in a heatproof bowl.
3. In a small saucepan, heat the condensed milk over low heat until warm but not boiling.
4. Pour the warm condensed milk over the chopped chocolate and let it sit for a minute.
5. Stir the mixture until the chocolate is completely melted and smooth.
6. **Add Champagne:**
7. Gently heat the champagne in a separate saucepan over low heat. Do not boil; just warm it.
8. Slowly pour the warm champagne into the chocolate mixture, stirring continuously until well combined.
9. **Chill the Mixture:**
10. Cover the mixture with plastic wrap, ensuring it directly touches the surface to prevent a skin from forming.
11. Refrigerate the mixture for at least 3-4 hours or until it's firm enough to handle.
12. **Shape Truffles:**
13. Once chilled, use a spoon to scoop out small portions and roll them into truffle-sized balls.
14. Place the truffles on a parchment-lined tray and return them to the fridge while you prepare the coating.
15. **Coat with Dark Chocolate:**
16. Melt a bit more dark chocolate in a heatproof bowl.
17. Dip each truffle into the melted chocolate, ensuring they are fully coated.
18. Place the coated truffles back on the parchment-lined tray.
19. **Decorate with Gold Leaf:**
20. Apply small pieces of edible gold leaf to the top of each truffle for a luxurious touch.
21. **Chill and Serve:**
22. Return the tray to the fridge to allow the chocolate coating to set completely.
23. Once set, remove the truffles from the fridge and dust them with cocoa powder.
24. **Serve and Indulge:**
25. Arrange the truffles on a beautiful serving plate and enjoy these Champagne and Gold Leaf Dark Chocolate Truffles, a truly decadent and luxurious treat.

Mooncakes

Ingredients

For the Shortbread:

- 2 cups all-purpose flour
- 1 cup unsalted butter, softened
- 1/2 cup powdered sugar
- 1 teaspoon vanilla extract

For the Blue Icing:

- 2 cups powdered sugar
- 2-3 tablespoons milk
- Blue food coloring

For the Golden Star Icing:

- 1/2 cup powdered sugar
- 1-2 tablespoons water
- Edible gold dust or food coloring

Cost
Medium

Time
6-9 Blocks

Difficulty
Medium

Introduction

Embark on a celestial journey — delicate shortbreads as if painted by the cosmos, each mooncake is a celebration of our destination . One that we may never reach, yet it's the tasty journey which makes each bite an otherworldly delight.

Method

1. Prepare the Shortbread:
   - In a bowl, cream together the softened butter and powdered sugar until light and fluffy. Add the vanilla extract and mix well. Gradually incorporate the flour until a soft dough forms.
   - Wrap the dough in plastic wrap and chill it in the refrigerator for at least 30 minutes.
2. Shape the Mooncakes:
   - Preheat the oven to 350°F (180°C). Roll out the chilled dough on a floured surface to about 1/4-inch thickness. Use a pastry-wheel on the edged, if you want to be fancy.
3. Bake:
   - Place the shaped mooncakes on a parchment-lined baking sheet and bake for 12-15 minutes or until the edges are lightly golden. Allow them to cool completely.
4. Prepare Blue Icing:
   - In a bowl, mix powdered sugar with milk to create a thick, yet pourable, icing consistency. Add blue food coloring until you achieve the desired hue.
5. Ice the Mooncakes:
   - Carefully spoon the blue icing over the cooled mooncakes, allowing it to drip down the sides.
6. Prepare Golden Star Icing:
   - Mix powdered sugar with water to create a thick icing. Add edible gold dust or gold food coloring until the icing achieves a rich golden color.
7. Decorate with Golden Stars:
   - Using a piping bag or a small spoon, create golden stars on top of the blue icing. You can also add small golden dots to enhance the celestial theme.
8. Let Set:
   - Allow the icing to set completely before serving or storing the mooncakes.
9. Celebrate the Journey:

- Enjoy these celestial delights with friends and family, savoring not just the taste but the imaginative journey each Mooncake represents.

Proof of Work

Ingredients

Ingredients:

- 1 cup water
- 1/2 cup unsalted butter
- 1/4 teaspoon salt
- 1 cup all-purpose flour
- 4 large eggs

For the Pastry Cream:

- 2 cups whole milk
- 1 vanilla bean, split and scraped (or 1 teaspoon vanilla extract)
- 6 large egg yolks
- 1/2 cup granulated sugar
- 1/3 cup cornstarch

For the Almond Toffee Lace:

- 1 cup granulated sugar
- 1/4 cup water
- 1 cup sliced almonds, toasted

Cost
Bear

Time
18 Blocks

Difficulty
ULTRA Difficult

Introduction

Inspired by the infamous MasterChef challenge that reduced contestants to tears, Ariano Zumbo's croquembouche (pronounced krok-em-boosh) captivated a nation, as participants faced the daunting tower with their hearts in their hands. Much like this laborious masterpiece, true cooking skills can't be faked; it's about putting in the work, showcasing competence, and thriving under pressure.

This tower stands as a testament to the skills you've acquired throughout this culinary journey. From reheating pizza in the bear market to crafting dishes of opulence in the bull, you've honed your abilities. The croquembouche is the ultimate test, separating the novices from the masters. Just as constructing this tower requires precision and attention to detail, so does navigating the world of Bitcoin. It's the final frontier where your skills and resilience are put to the ultimate test.

Remember, this isn't just about food any more, we've well and truely passed that; this is your crossing of the rubicon and your stance of rebellion. Arm yourself with a saucepan and brace for the giant challenge ahead, for things are about to get nuts. We're cooking for freedom, we're cooking for revolution and we're cooking with Bitcoin.

Method

Pastry Cream:

1. In a saucepan, heat the milk with the vanilla bean (or extract) until it just begins to boil. Remove from heat.
2. In a bowl, whisk together the egg yolks, sugar, and cornstarch until smooth.
3. Slowly pour the hot milk into the egg mixture, whisking continuously.
4. Return the mixture to the saucepan and cook over medium heat, stirring constantly until it thickens.
5. Once thickened, strain the pastry cream into a bowl, cover with plastic wrap (directly on the surface), and chill in the refrigerator.

Cont.

Choux Pastry:

1. Preheat the oven to 425°F (220°C). Line a baking sheet with parchment paper.
2. In a saucepan, combine water, butter, and salt. Bring to a boil.
3. Remove from heat and quickly stir in the flour until the mixture forms a ball.
4. Transfer the dough to a mixing bowl. Add eggs one at a time, beating well after each addition.
5. Transfer the dough to a piping bag fitted with a large round tip. Pipe small mounds onto the prepared baking sheet.
6. Bake for 15-20 minutes until golden brown. Let cool.

Assembly:

1. Fill each pastry puff with the prepared pastry cream using a piping bag.
2. Dip the tops of the filled puffs into the almond toffee, then stack them to form a cone or tower.
3. Drizzle any remaining toffee over the tower and allow it to set.
4. Optionally, decorate the tower with spun sugar or edible flowers.

If you've made it this far, sit back, wipe those tears away and marvel at your creation. Your eyes will forever have a laserish orange hue, and your soverignty is yours. You are a Bitcoin chef.

Join the revolution...

There are the 'Fiat Chefs,' and then there's us.

Simply picking up this book is a testament to your freedom-loving spirit. Once you start cooking with that mindset, taste breaks free, leaving the bland flavors of fiat-based dishes in the past.

Bitcoin and Food form the ideal pairing, and your culinary creations with this book are at the forefront of that revolution.

However, a revolution can't thrive in silence. Share your incredible dishes on social media — hashtag each recipe with **#CookingWithBitcoin**

This book is more than just recipes; it's about the technology that has the power to free us. Embrace Satoshi's discovery, cook with Bitcoin in your heart, and showcase what you've created to the world!

The most exceptional Bitcoin-based meals will be highlighted on the site, potentially showcased in an upcoming book, and serve as the tasty fuel for the ongoing revolution as we propel ourselves forward.

Don't sit back, and just praise Bitcoin from the sidelines, pick up a spatula and start cooking! Invite your friends over to savor your crypto carbonara, your lemon ledgers, your Satoshi salad, or even your Proof of Work croquembouche!

Join the challenge of serving up these tasty ideas. Look beyond the cheesy names and truly take part in what we're cooking up — a revolution.
Your secret ingredient... Bitcoin.

#CookingWithBitcoin

Follow Me

annaanon.com

@ChefAnnaAnon @ChefAnnaAnon @ChefAnnaAnon

Printed in Dunstable, United Kingdom

91335492R00092